Fueled by Purpose

A Journey of Grit and Growth

Kal Patel

ISBN: 979-8-89663-770-7

Dedication

To my mom in heaven, whose love and guidance continue to inspire me every day.

Acknowledgment

To my amazing wife, Lina, and my beautiful daughters, Dharma and Saiya, for your endless love, support, and encouragement.

To my family for always standing by my side through every joy and challenge.

To my friends and partners for always being there, encouraging me, and believing in me.

And to my mentor, Craig Auberger, for your unwavering guidance and belief in me.

Thank you all for being there for me and supporting me both mentally and physically. I wouldn't be where I am today without each of you, and I'm so grateful to share this journey with everyone reading this.

About the Author

When I reflect on my journey, I see a story of grit, perseverance, and passion that transformed challenges into opportunities. From my early days as a dreamer with a vision to becoming the founder and CEO of multiple companies, I've navigated the intricate landscapes of entrepreneurship within multiple industries.

My expertise isn't just theoretical; it's rooted in real-world achievements, from scaling ventures to redefining industries. I have led efforts to bring hospitality principles into healthcare, combining service excellence with patient-centered care. My entrepreneurial career spans real estate, development, construction, hospitality, healthcare, social media ad agency, and franchise ownership, all underpinned by a drive to transform ideas into impactful realities.

I've shared these insights as a featured speaker at platforms like Inspection Fuel, Mason Made Chamber Annual Summit, and the Indian American Chamber of Commerce, inspiring business leaders to embrace innovative strategies. As a member of the Forbes Business Development Council and an Entrepreneur Leadership Network Contributor, I've worked to inspire others to push beyond boundaries.

This book isn't just about what I've achieved; it's about how you can use these principles to achieve your own dreams. Whether you're starting out or seeking a fresh perspective, my hope is to inspire you to embrace challenges and turn them into stepping stones for success.

Contents

Chapter 1: The Beginning

Perhaps the best and most concise way life is summed up by Frank Sinatra in his song, "That's Life."

"...You're flying high in April; shot down in May.

But I know I'm gonna change that tune,

When I'm back on top, back on top in June..."

Regardless of where you're born or even the situation you were born into, it all boils down to what you do with it. Unless you were born with a silver spoon in your mouth, you wouldn't understand how necessary this "hustle" is.

My name's Kalpesh Patel and this is the story of my entrepreneurial journey!

My father was born in Raipur, a busy city in the province of Uttar Pradesh, India. His life was challenging from the get-go. His father died when he was only a year old. My grandfather owned two businesses, a lumber mill, and two movie theaters, both in partnerships with his associates. Unfortunately for my father, his business associates managed to coerce and bribe government officials, and my dad's family lost all ownership. Laws and rules were somewhat lax back then. If you had enough money and knew the right people, the laws always worked in your favor.

My grandmother, who was now a widow, moved in with her brother. She raised my aunt and my father at her brother's house in Vadhvania. They ended up living there for

15 years. By the time my father turned 16, his family had saved up enough money to buy a small house and a few acres of land. The house cost 3,000 rupees, and the land cost 7,500 – a mere 10,500 rupees to have a fresh start in life. The land was used for growing simple crops, like cotton and certain types of beans. They weren't too challenging to grow and provided a modest income.

My father realized the importance of education from an early age. Working tirelessly on the farms allowed him to save up enough money to attain further education. Public schools had a minimal monthly fee, which was relatively easy to pay. His high school was in the small town of Kadod, where he studied up till the 12th grade.

Since my father was the "man of the house," he had to support his mother and sister. To do this, not only did my father have to study further, but he also had to learn a vocational skill that could help bring in additional income quicker. He went to a college in Baroda (now named Vadodara) to do a year-long electrician course. Knowing that wouldn't be enough, he did a drawing and typing course alongside it, as well. This allowed him to not only support his family but also save up enough money to pursue higher education.

At the age of 21, he went to college in Vallabh Vidyanagar. He graduated four years later with his general studies degree. He planned on continuing his education and moving on to study law. Seeing the state of law and order in India at the time, he wanted to contribute to a positive change. However, his uncle managed to convince him to get married first.

My mother's brother-in-law introduced my father to her back in 1965. They got along well, and their marriage was quickly arranged. My mother only studied until high school, which was considered more than enough for a woman. It was the norm at the time. In 1966, my parents moved to Bardoli. However, my grandmother didn't want to leave her village, so she ended up staying there.

In Bardoli, my father opened up an engineering workshop. His firm made parts for diamond-cutting machines. He started this business under a partnership, which, unfortunately, did not turn out the way he planned. My father was a simple, straightforward man, unaware of the clever tactics that people used. He was tricked into selling off his shares, from which he got no profits – just like what happened to his father before. This landed an immense blow to him, both mentally and financially. My father had no other choice but to move back in with his mother.

Perhaps this was the turning point for him. He realized how most of the problems he faced throughout his life were caused by dishonest people. He was also affected by the lack of accountability by the police and the judiciary. My father realized to actually live an honest life – where he could make something of himself – he would have to leave India and start life somewhere fresh. He decided on the U.S.!

Even though most of his education was in Hindi, he still understood a decent amount of English. It wouldn't be enough for the U.S., but it was a start. He worked tirelessly on the farm to save up to make a move. All of his efforts were ultimately for his family.

In 1972, he finally got a chance. My father was offered an opportunity to move to the U.S. via Canada. He managed to save up to 5,000 rupees, and he borrowed another 5,000 rupees from his uncle to buy a ticket to go to Canada. I was only six months old when he moved to Toronto, where he lived in a small apartment with a few other friends who took this leap of faith with him. My father worked long hours at a local pizza parlor just so he could save up enough money to buy our tickets. So, the rest of us could move to Toronto, too.

This was an especially trying time for my mother. "International calls" were the epitome of luxury at the time – something we couldn't afford. Most of the communication was done via handwritten letters. It was tough for her, but she realized that my father's sacrifice was ultimately for our better future.

By the time I turned two, my father had managed to save enough money so we could move to Canada. Both of my parents had to work to provide for us. They also had to save up so we could eventually move to the U.S.

My father had this innate sense of entrepreneurship, something he got from my grandfather. Both of them started their businesses and were quite successful. The only thing that was a hurdle in their paths was dishonest business partners. My father was resilient – "giving up" was never in his dictionary. Even though Canada was nice, my father realized he could make a better future for his family in the U.S., which, at the time, was developing much more rapidly than Canada. Both of them were determined to bring their plans to fruition, and they were willing to do anything it took for us.

Migration is perhaps one of the most challenging things a person can endure. Leaving behind your home, family, and friends and going to another country – where they don't even speak the same language as you – are quite strong hurdles. Back then, people weren't as accepting as they are now, which created problems of their own.

My parents left everything behind just so we could have a chance at living a better life. They faced some of the toughest challenges you could throw at someone. They did it while smiling, just for us, so we have a better chance at life.

I'm at a loss for words when it comes to describing how much I love my parents. I couldn't even hold a candle to their sacrifices for us. My parents are absolutely terrific! Believe me when I say I wouldn't be half the person I am if it weren't for their ceaseless efforts. I love you, Mom and Dad. Thank you for all your love and support!

"The first step towards getting somewhere is to decide that you are not going to stay where you are."

-JP Morgan

Chapter 2: Moving to the USA

Our parents dedicated their blood, sweat, and tears to us so that we could have the basic necessities of life. It seemed like our situation would never change - a constant battle of making ends meet- when one day, we finally received good news. As it turned out, we happened to have some distant relatives who moved not too long ago to Wilmington, California. Those relatives of ours happened to be much better off than we were, and they managed to establish their own motel. That motel was wildly successful and brought hope to my parents; if they can do it, so can we.

My parents were convinced. Thus, taking a leap of faith, they poured in whatever money they had managed to save, along with loans from friends and family. Back then, real estate wasn't nearly as expensive as it is now, and we barely managed to afford it. This was a considerable risk, as either everything was to go swimmingly or *all* the money my parents invested would go to waste, and we would have ended up bankrupt under piles of debt.

Fortunately, the risk paid off as the Patels became the proud owners of the Monterey Inn in Wilmington, California. The distant relatives who had their motel were living here, and they helped us a great deal.

Even after all these years, I have vivid memories of my early childhood spent running around our motel's hallways, playing hide and seek with my siblings while trying my best not to annoy the customers. The front desk was on the second floor. It had a Dutch door, so you could open just the top portion and negotiate with the guests.

All of us were staying in one room. As you walked in, you would see a small kitchen to your right. I have many beautiful memories of my mother cooking us traditional Indian food; the aroma would fill our room and only makes our mouths water more. There was only one bedroom and one bathroom in this room with a small lounge.

In our small apartment/reception, all six of us would huddle together. My parents made makeshift beds in the lounge by putting down some bed sheets on the floor and slept there. My brother, sister, grandmother, and I would all sleep in the bedroom. It got rather cramped at times, but if anything, it made us value the importance of family; *we were everything we had in this country.* This taught us how to make the best of every situation and be grateful for whatever we had.

My sister is the oldest of us three siblings. In many ways, she did a lot of "mom" work while our parents were busy. She would look after us while our parents worked and made snacks for my brother and me every day after school. We never really had many toys, to begin with, so we found whatever we could around the motel to pass the time with: pillow forts, a small "metropolis" made of empty shampoo bottles, a mattress jumping castle, the works.

Our *MacGyver*-style games managed to create a lot of havoc. Perhaps one of the worst instances of this was when we found an old shopping cart and made a game out of it.

We flipped it upside down, with me "caged" inside. I pretended to be a dog, barking at my siblings if they came close. Whenever I would try to come out of this "cage," they would drop the gate of the cart, forcing me to stay inside. We did this a handful of times; it was ridiculously fun. However, as they slammed the gate down on the fourth attempt, I couldn't move my hand back in fast enough. In the process, my pinky got in the way and ended up getting cut nearly through – barely dangling on by a piece of skin. My siblings were terrified by this sight, and they ran and hid behind a dumpster. I rushed back into the motel, holding my dangling pinky in place, all the while howling in agony. It took my parents a minute to register what happened as they saw me with blood dripping from my finger and all over my shirt. Naturally, my mom freaked out. However, my dad stayed very calm and collected and took me to the emergency room.

I ended up having to wait nearly four hours in the musty waiting lobby before a doctor arrived and examined my pinky. He very nonchalantly informed me that there was nothing that could be done – my pinky would just have to be amputated. This, of course, was petrifying. As my father tried to console me, trying to convince me that a life without all ten digits was fairly common, a doctor/angel came up to us. He examined my pinky and reassured me that he would be able to reattach it, the only drawback being that my fingernail may never grow back again. I opted for this, obviously – no nail is much better than no finger. After a small surgery, I was good to go. To my surprise, my nail did grow back after a few months, leaving me with just a small scar now.

We may not have had enough space in our apartment, but we sure as hell had enough room in our hearts! When my siblings and I were headed out to school one day, we found a puppy outside the motel. It was very small and ridiculously cute; I would be lying if I said I didn't immediately fall in love with it! We brought it back inside and asked our parents if we could keep it. Our parents' response was rather unenthusiastic. They didn't agree to keep the puppy, and instead, our mother scolded us for being late for school. I still remember the three of us walking to school, teary-eyed because we wouldn't be able to keep the puppy.

However, things turned out for the best! When we came back home, our initial dread immediately turned into excitement as we heard the puppy squealing. We began searching through the motel, running around the hallways and checking every nook and cranny, till I finally found him hidden in the cabinet under the sink in our kitchen. Our parents had heard our pleas and allowed us to keep the puppy! They bathed it and fed him. We ended up naming him Max.

I later learned that we ended up keeping the puppy because my father used to have one growing up. He had a German shepherd he raised since it was a puppy. In many ways, he emphasized the importance of owning a pet from a young age as it taught responsibility. As it turned out, having Max around really helped us later in life. We catered to his needs the best we could, and with enough training, he was an obedient and well-behaved dog. As Max was a German shepherd as well, it didn't take him long to grow exponentially in size. This was useful for multiple reasons. As time went on, the occurrences of "rough" guests increased.

Perhaps one of the worst incidents of this was when one of these guests, who was quite clearly intoxicated, tried to assault my father physically. He managed to grab my father by the collar from the Dutch door and almost punched him, but Max took no time at all to react and immediately jumped through the opening and bit the assailant. Max was able to hold him off long enough for the police to show up and diffuse the situation. If it weren't for Max, my father would have been badly injured that day.

As much as I would have loved to have Max around, regrettably, he died a year after that incident; he got hit by a car and died. It was a somber day for all of us, and we still talk about him in conversation now and then. The type of dog Max was made me realize dogs are a man's best friend.

After a few more unscrupulous events at the motel, my parents decided it would be best if we moved somewhere quieter; they agreed on Oklahoma. We had family friends in Oklahoma who had established themselves in the hospitality business. We took a long road trip, driving 6-7 hours a day. Nearly every motel we stopped at happened to be owned by our parents' friends and distant relatives from India. We would spend a night with them on our stops. They treated us like family, and their exceptional hospitality is something I hold dear even to this day.

Since most of the places we stopped at were motels, I noticed how Indians owned nearly all of them. My dad explained why this was the case. Everyone from our state of Gujarat, where he grew up, was a landowner. They had lots of land for themselves where they did various agricultural things. Here, in the U.S., they were motel owners, still landowners, just with a different purpose for it.

My father had managed to find a 30-room motel up for sale, the Key Motel. He put down the deposit for it before we arrived. When we got there, we were shocked; the entire motel was badly vandalized. There was profane graffiti, broken windows, and most of the furniture and electronics from the rooms were stolen. This wasn't very comforting to all of us. We would have to forfeit a lot of money we worked very hard on.

This was the time my father decided to take a drastic measure. He thought it best that we are raised far away from the major cities, somewhere quiet. After going through countless classifieds, he finally found a small town in Oklahoma – Vinita. The population was a mere 7000, and it seemed like the perfect place for us to start fresh once again.

We had lost a considerable amount of money from our previous investment. As such, we could only afford a small, 16-room motel in Vinita called the Prairie Schooner Motel. The owner financed the motel, so my dad was able to pay for a small down payment, and we moved in soon after. By now, we were a bit older and could actively participate in the motel's upkeep. We began to live a wonderful life in a wonderful town. The motel may not have had many rooms, but it had several acres of adjoining land. The "backyard" was over four acres. It had lots of different fruit trees, grapevines, and vegetables as far as the eye could see. My grandmother would always be in the gardens at all hours of the day. She taught me how to plant vegetables and how to tend to them – proper growing techniques, so we had enough for ourselves and to give to our friends and family. This was what she did growing up and is what her parents taught her. She wasn't just passing down skills, but there was a deeper life lesson in all of this – take care of yourself and others.

All three of us siblings would wake up at 6 a.m. every day. We would clean out the rooms that had checked out from the night before, take out the garbage, and put the dirty sheets and dirty towels in the laundry. We did all of these errands daily before we got ready and went to school.

My parents taught us the ins and outs of many different skills. We learned about housekeeping, maintenance, landscaping – you name it, we did it. As we got older, we learned more technical skills, such as putting on metal roofs, painting the motel's interior and exterior, and even blacktopping the asphalt in the parking lot. My parents always emphasized the importance of working hard, but they emphasized more on *working smart.*

As important as it was to be hardworking, it was equally important to know when to kick back and relax. We would always make time for a family vacation, often going to Florida or hanging out at our friends' houses. Perhaps my favorite memory of those vacations we took was the Will Rogers Memorial Rodeo. We would enjoy the rodeo's spectacle and indulge ourselves in the various types of activities involved. They would have eight exciting events held every night for four consecutive nights: barrel racing, bronc riding, team roping, steer wrestling, saddle bronc riding, bull riding, calf roping, and steer roping. We would watch the rodeo and eat the various types of delicious food available at our disposal; funnel cakes were my personal favorite.

This was around the time when I learned the skill of customer service. I learned how to negotiate with customers, how to rent rooms, and provide an overall wonderful experience to all of our customers – irrespective of who they were. The announcers at the rodeo showcased their masterful showmanship, and I absorbed all of that like a sponge – hospitality became a part of my DNA.

I began to understand how vital it was to communicate with all types of people, irrespective of their age. The goal was to deliver a fantastic service to our guests so they would remember our motel the next time they needed a place to stay. Vinita was a very quaint town; everyone knew each other. I believe this was one of the reasons why my parents loved Vinita so much; it reminded them of the close-knit communities the people in the villages back in India had.

"We need to find ways to come together and build community because when we do, we can accomplish anything."

-Michelle Obama

Chapter 3: Becoming an Entrepreneur in Middle School

It has been three months since I started listening to Bohemian Rhapsody by Queen on repeat:

So you think you can stone me and spit in my eye?

So you think you can love me and leave me to die?

Oh, baby, can't do this to me, baby,

Just gotta get out, just gotta get right outta here.

We had a black 8-track player in the motel's lobby. I indistinctly used to tell myself life is going to get better. Later, it became a practice. Everybody has ups and downs in life. And I knew this wasn't anything but a phase that would eventually fade into thin air. I believe that time heals everything.

School life was quite challenging. The obscurity of the discrimination that I feared under my skin became perceivable. I was in second grade when I first started school in Vinita, Oklahoma. At first, it felt peculiarly different. I was the only Indian kid in my grade. These kids had never met a person outside of the United States. To be fair, it was a tough adjustment that I had to make. The first question the kids asked me was:

"Which tribe do you belong to?"

To which I used to respond by saying, "I am from India," innocently.

They were flabbergasted by my existence. They gawked at me like a hawk for the next couple of months until they got comfortable with my presence. They even ridiculed me for the culture my family brought along, especially the food we consumed.

These were during the times when multiple businesses had signs outside their business that said, 'American Owned.' I was too young to understand the meaning and resolution behind these signs and the verbiage written on them. However, as I grew up, I introduced myself to the true concept of discrimination. This was all too disappointing for me. This conflicted with the image of the United States I had in my mind. At that time, I realized if you are an outsider, you will be looked down upon as a foreigner. Even though my family was 'American,' people weren't ready to accept that.

Nevertheless, with time, people progressed and changed. Despite all the turmoil that we encountered, we readjusted ourselves in this old world with new people. In this phase of life, I learned that people are tough to convince. Deep down, we all are bigots. However, we began to educate others on our culture and traditions. We made them understand that we were precisely the same as them. We were just originally from another culture. Eventually, they started respecting our values.

In school, I ended up making a few friends. I also learned that good and bad people are everywhere in this world. It is only a matter of who we choose to be around. Most people ridiculed my background. In that crowd of people, a group of people accepted me for who I was. This is how this realization came to me. I made some really good friends in elementary and high school, who eventually became my best buddies. They were amazing people. Even after all these years, I am still in contact with them. To this date, they are the same as they were back in school.

Living in a motel wasn't easy. I never had the liberty to invite my friends over to play and hang out. It was a business. Our presence would have disturbed the guests staying there. Even my parents didn't allow me to bring friends over. As a solution, we used to take our bikes and go out. We would either visit my friends' homes or go somewhere else in the town unless it was too cold. In winter, I used to invite them over to have cocoa and play cards.

Adjusting to these things helped me navigate challenging situations in life when I became an adult. I believe the way I was forced to look at life offered a somewhat interesting perspective that fate awarded me with. I grew up learning a lot of things about people and the trials of life. For me, it was an early maturing phase, and I am more than grateful for that.

I envied the opulent lifestyle that my friends were blessed with. I used to listen to their stories about what they did all day. Unlike me, they didn't have to work in a business. They did their house chores and then relaxed after school. Meanwhile, I was assigned multiple chores at the motel before and after school that I had to do. It was all too frustrating for me, so I started complaining. I complained a lot. One day, my father had enough of me. He told me I could move out and live with my friends if I didn't like helping around in the motel. Honestly, I thought about it, but I didn't do it. At that time, I didn't know the lessons my parents taught us would help us learn work ethics and build a character that later helped me.

Sports have played a significant role in my life. It helped me value the meaning of teamwork. I learned there is no victory without teamwork. I enjoyed all types of athletic activities, but among those, I absolutely loved playing soccer with my friends in school. My parents couldn't take me to the games with all the burdens they had on their shoulders. They told me I could continue playing, only if I could find myself a ride back home. Consequently, I ended up quitting the league. Still, I continued to play it with my friends in their backyards.

I always had a third eye for arts and crafts. I desperately used to wait for the art class. I learned to paint and also played with ceramics. My art and craft teacher was a wonderful lady who encouraged kids to be the best version of themselves. Even outside the school, I would go home and practice my skills. Eventually, it became a hobby. To this day, I still paint big canvases and decorate the walls with my work, which I am proud of.

When it came to academics, I loved mathematics and was naturally good at it. Solutions to challenging problems would eventually come to my mind. At the same time, I contended with science. As a kid, I wished science was as easy as mathematics was for me, but it was tough. I barely used to score a 'C' in it. I realized the things that I enjoyed were easy, and the things that I didn't enjoy were hard. This helped me understand the fundamental code of indulging in something. After that, I made sure I enjoyed everything I did.

In middle school, my parents used to give me $2 for lunch every day. It was a fair amount that all the other kids used to get, as well. I was tired of eating the same lunch every day, so I started saving my daily pocket money instead of spending it. I starved myself in school. I used to kill time sitting in the cafeteria reading a book during lunch and saved $10 by the end of the week. Next week, I ordered a pepperoni pizza and had it delivered to the school on Monday. My intentions were clear, and I didn't mean to make a business out of it. However, during lunch, my peer group came running to me when they saw me with a pizza. Everyone asked if they could have a slice of it. I was generous and offered everyone a slice for $2. I ended up selling all 10 slices and made $20.00. I made $10.00 extra on the total. I was proud of myself and happy because I helped my friends out. Like me, they were tired of the same food every day, too. This is how I started making $40 by just selling pizza in school every week. Eventually, I stopped asking for money from my parents and started to take care of my expenses. This was the first step that I took toward becoming an entrepreneur.

In high school, I took a wood workshop and learned to make different wooden artifacts. I was always challenged by my will to try new things. I made a three-tier potato and onion stand back then. I spent several months working on it. It filled me with delight when I brought it home to my parents. They appreciated me for my hard work and encouraged me to keep up with my endeavors. Even after all these years, my parents still have that stand in their house. Whenever I look at it, I always zone out back to those halcyon days.

These things have helped me understand and deal with the challenges that I later faced in my life. The things that I self-taught myself and the sanctions that my parents had me under were not associated with any of the traditional classes we attended in school. Learning to cook, sew, clean, and organize stuff has helped me become who I am today. These things even aided me in finding solutions to the trials that life threw at me.

Apart from the usual, I was a bit troublesome, as well. I was known as the class clown. I used to make the entire class laugh by pulling pranks on the teachers and other kids. I was quite fond of keeping it lighthearted in school. I can still envision the day before my high school graduation when we all were busy decorating for our big day. My school principal, who was a nice man, came to my best friend and me and warned us, 'If you both pull any prank during graduation, you will not graduate."

Along with mathematics and arts, I undoubtedly enjoyed being goofy. I believed in being a part of the community, team, and school. Therefore, I lived by only one motto, i.e., "Enjoy life to the fullest."

Anything I did, I made sure to have fun doing it. I was in the class of 90, and looking back, I have many cherished memories, like going to Junior and Senior Prom and participating in pep rallies. However, my brother and sister always averted from the activities I indulged in. I believe they feared something. I still don't know what it was, but my parents were impressed. They often used to ask me, "Why do you have to do all these things? Why can you not be like your brother and sister?" In my world, I wanted to be the authentic version of myself. I was fearless! I was always ready to explore and try new things. My first paid job was at The World's Largest McDonald's at that time. I started by working in the back, making fries, flipping burgers, stocking, mopping floors, and all for $1.85 per hour. I remember working long hours after school and on the weekends, moving up within a few months to a cashier, and getting a few raises throughout. I ended up making about $2.25 per hour. I was constantly asking questions and learning about the business, customer service, and supervisory skills so that I could have personal growth.

As an adult, when I look back at my life, I am always moved. How it changed in the blink of an eye is still an enigma that I cannot decipher! It was quite interesting for me to realize that all the different things we learn from middle school to high school later serve a purpose in our lives. When I started selling pizza back in the 7th grade, I didn't understand my 'entrepreneurship' skills. It was a talent and a business mindset that I possessed all this time. Years have passed, and sitting by this fireplace in the cold winter, I cannot thank God enough for where I am today. The way life suddenly yet inevitably starts maneuvering is a dilemma that I think I will never be able to comprehend.

This same song that I am still listening to has come to an end:

'Nothing really matters,

Anyone can see,

Nothing really matters,

Nothing really matters to me.'

I just want to say. 'To strive, you must struggle in life.'

"The individual has always had to struggle to keep from being overwhelmed by the tribe. If you try it, you will be lonely often and sometimes frightened. But no price is too high to pay for the privilege of owning yourself."

- Friedrich Nietzsche

Chapter 4: The College Years

After finishing high school in 1990, I decided to go to Northeastern Oklahoma A&M College, a small public Community College in Miami, Oklahoma, which is about 30 miles away from my hometown Vinita. The Golden Norseman was the school's mascot because the ferocious Norsemen warriors from Europe resonated with the soaring spirits of the college in 1945.

My high school buddy and I got an apartment and started our first year of college. My parents really wanted me to go into the medical field, but I didn't want to be a doctor. So, I decided to pursue dentistry instead, but when I went to shadow a dentist in my first year, I quickly discovered that I really couldn't see myself working in a small four-square-inch area for hours at a time.

After that realization, I decided to go into business and ended up majoring in marketing with management as my minor. I didn't actually have the heart to tell my parents about my academic pursuits because I knew that they would be disappointed. Most of their friends' children were going into either medicine, engineering, or law. My sister had enrolled in a medical college, and my brother had gone to school for engineering, honoring my parents' wishes. I felt like a black sheep going against their wishes when my parents were working really hard to make sure my brother, sister, and I had all the things we needed to go to school and become successful.

They eventually bought a second motel in town about five miles away from the original motel. It was the "Holiday Motel" and had about 25 rooms and an outdoor pool. My dad stayed at the one motel out of town, and my mom stayed at the one in town. Seeing them work so hard to support us financially made it difficult for me to tell my parents that I didn't want to be a doctor and wanted to go into business instead; I couldn't disappoint them.

Even now, when I think about it, I can't believe the lengths my parents went to provide for us. Anyway, despite my appreciation for everything they did for me, I just couldn't tell them that I was not going to go into the medical field. By that time, I had built up my credit because of the jobs and starting college. As a result, I started getting a lot of credit card applications that amazed me. In excitement, I applied for many of the cards and started buying silly things like speakers, the stereo system, and new windows for my car. And that was just the start! I also had a girlfriend at the time, so I decided to buy her some gifts.

We would go out for dinner every other night and just enjoy life, all on credit. They didn't really tell you how to manage money or credit cards in high school, so I had no idea what I was doing. Soon, I was working more hours to pay off the credit cards and was falling behind in school. My grades weren't the best even before the credit situation as I had always struggled to manage work with studies; still, I had decent grades, and I managed to keep my budget somewhat under control, but that didn't last when debt piled up.

My grades continued to drop, and I kept trying to work more to pay off the credit cards, but I didn't do a really good job, and soon, I was in over my head. I had stopped making credit card payments, and my credit started getting really bad, but I kept thinking that everything would be okay and this would all work itself out. It really hurts me to think that I was taking advantage of the difficulties my parents went through; I had the opportunity to go to college and make progress, but I was wasting it away by going out there and living a fun life when it should have been more focused on learning and getting my college degree.

During that first year of college, I would go back home once a month and visit my friends from high school and family. But during the time I wouldn't go home, I would get together with my roommates and friends, and we would watch some football games and have parties at our apartment when we weren't studying.

That actually led to our apartment becoming the hub for social gatherings, which did not help me with staying focused on school. I wish I had realized then that I needed to focus more on school rather than socializing so much; it would have solved a lot of the problems that I would encounter in the future.

My roommate was one of my high school friends, so we got along very well because we used to hang out during high school. The first year of college still felt like being in high school, except I had much more freedom and what I thought were fewer responsibilities. But in hindsight, I really wish I had a mentor or coach who would have helped me understand and navigate the college years. I finished up my first year at A&M and then decided to transfer to the University of Oklahoma as I always wanted to go there. I had two other roommates who were friends of mine, so we decided to rent a house and live together. I started attending classes and going to work, and naturally, things got better for me as I focused on my school and tried to manage my finances better.

To my surprise, I was really enjoying my classes geared toward marketing and management. One of my favorite classes was advertising, and one of the most memorable assignments that we had was to come up with a video advertisement. It involved coming up with a script and participating as actors; all the ads were to be voted on by our classmates or peers for mark distribution. Our group spent several weeks working on that assignment and was placed first out of six groups.

I worked at a local mall when I was in school, and during my college years, I worked at a retail clothing store where I became kind of a fashion consultant. I got paid on an hourly basis plus commission, and I would always be at the top of the salespeople in the store. I think that goes back to me always being very social and trying to take care of the needs of others. I would always look at what the customers were trying to achieve and then come up with the best solution.

One of my other jobs was working at a sales call center, selling long-distance plans. I remember hitting the quota very early in my shifts because of my ability to discover what the potential customer needed and find a solution for their needs.

Now, don't get me wrong, because that wasn't all there was to my life, as I did some fun stuff. I went to many tailgate parties as the Oklahoma Sooners were and still are one of the best college football teams. I became very close with some people during my time here, and we would participate in many social activities and clubs.

As the years went by, I still found myself getting caught up in partying and socializing too much, and my grades weren't quite where they needed to be. I realized once again that not preparing for a bad spell was one of my biggest pitfalls.

I would strongly advise young people who are in high school to reach out and find a mentor or coach who can help them understand and navigate the importance of staying focused and teach them how to manage their time and money. During my years at OU, I would go home once every couple of months. Around the same time, my parents had to let the motel in town go because it wasn't doing well financially. I can't reiterate how much hurt I feel today, knowing that I was not taking full advantage of my college years back then when my parents were struggling to make ends meet.

I continued to study at OU for the next two years, and then I decided to move to Stillwater, where my brother had gone to school. I thought I would try to go to school there for a year, but that didn't quite go exactly how I wanted. Instead, I worked for a year while staying at a family friend's motel.

They took me in as one of their own and tried to help me the best they could. They were always making food for me and tried their hardest to make me feel at home. I would go as far as saying that they were like a second set of parents for me there. I really didn't know a lot of people there and spent most of the time just working and staying in the motel room. I did, however, end up meeting a friend who hung out with me; we would go to work out and socialize a little bit. He was actually one of the primary reasons that I was able to meet my wife, which I'll get into a little more detail later.

After one year of staying in Stillwater, I moved to Lawton, Oklahoma, to attend Cameron University. I really wanted to focus and be done with school this time around. When I first moved to Lawton, I stayed with some family friends who opened up their home and their lives to me as if I were family.

I am always going to be grateful for all they did for me. I worked a lot during my college years, and while working, I discovered that nothing in life had prepared me for college and its education system. Everything that I learned during my college years was through real-life experiences that I gathered in the workforce that helped me discover myself.

I had several jobs during my college years, and most of them were in the retail industry, which made me realize that I enjoyed working with people and taking care of them and their needs. I also helped out the family friends I stayed with by working at the front desk, housekeeping, or doing whatever else they needed my help with. While I was staying at their places, everything seemed to be about hospitality and taking care of people.

Aside from work and studies, I spent a lot of time on the phone, calling my wife-to-be and visiting her frequently during this time as she lived in Dyersburg, Tennessee. I struggled with school till the very end and was never able to finish it. I do regret not getting my bachelor's degree, but the lessons that I learned during those times would significantly impact me in the years that were to come. Again, I can't stress the importance of getting a mentor or a coach to help navigate these times enough because they're very challenging times, which I obviously didn't realize at the time.

"I encourage all of you to seek out teachers and mentors that challenge you to think for yourself and guide you to find your own voice."

-Renee Olstead

Chapter 5: Getting Married: A New Beginning

Life unfolds in phases, each teaching us about relationships, people, and places. Entering a meaningful relationship is like discovering a connection, blending similarities with intriguing differences. My journey into this phase began in October 1994.

One day, while hanging out with a friend, he mentioned a girl he'd been chatting with—a girl with a Southern accent who'd lived in Tennessee. Later, while we were out, he handed me the phone unexpectedly.

"Hey! It's Kalpesh," I said nervously.

"Hello Kalpesh, how are you?" she replied, calm and confident.

Explaining why I had the phone, I tried to keep the conversation flowing. Her name was Lina. Though I'd never spoken to her before, I found her engaging and grounded. We talked easily, and our chat left a lasting impression.

A few days later, my friend brought her up again, which piqued my interest. Eventually, I got her number and started calling her after finishing my work quota at my telemarketing job. Long-distance calls were expensive, so work became my excuse to connect. Lina was different—her personality and values drew me in. She wasn't just kind; she was thoughtful, family-oriented, and spiritual, often talking about self-control and discipline.

As the eldest sibling, she carried a strong sense of responsibility, caring for her younger siblings when her parents were away. I, on the other hand, was the youngest and a little spoiled, so her maturity impressed me. Despite these differences, we shared similar views about life and ambitions. Conversations about work, education, and social issues strengthened our growing bond.

We gradually discovered each other's interests, ambitions, wants, and preferences. This formed the basis of a strong friendship that I thought would have developed until now. I wanted to see Lina, so I asked her to send me her picture through the mail and promised her I would send mine as well. I sent her one of my best pictures and then received mail from her. I was excited to know how she looked, and the moment I opened the envelope, I saw a young and beautiful girl who was only 8 or 9 years of age in that picture, standing in a garden wearing adorable apparel.

It was clear that she was uneasy about sharing her personal images with a stranger. This made me respect her more because she seemed a careful and vigilant girl. I wanted to meet her in person instead of asking for her updated picture to be sent again. I'm certain that it would be crazily insane and weird of me if I had done that.

While I was attending a wedding in Ohio, I met her sister, Kate. Her charm mirrored Lina's and reinforced my admiration for her family. That's when I decided I had to go meet Lina in person, and so I drove from Ohio to Memphis to meet her for the first time.

Our first meeting in person was magical. We went to see The Lion King at a theater. When I saw her for the first time, her smile lit up the room. Nervous energy filled the air, but we enjoyed our time together. During the movie, I playfully took her ring, and she called me later, telling me she thought she lost her ring. I told her I had it and that I would return it when we met again—ensuring our next meeting.

Afterward, when I came back home, she asked me to share my social security number with her, and I thought, why? She explained that she was concerned about hanging out with someone who might have a criminal record. As I mentioned above, Lina was quite a sane person who never wanted to take risks where there was ultimate danger. And to be honest, I liked this trait of her as well.

Anyway, I agreed to her request, thinking that's great and, above all, very smart of her. With each passing day, things got clearer, and I started seeing her on weekends when I had the time to see her; we used to have a great time together. Every time I went on to meet her, I bought roses and a stuffed toy.

One day, we met at an Indian wedding, and fortunately, both of her parents and my mom and sister were there as well. We introduced ourselves to them for the first time. It was a short meeting, but at least we were able to meet. Her mom knew we were traveling to Atlanta and would be passing by their town, so she invited us to stop by when we were on our way back home.

I remember calling Lina before we left Atlanta to head back to Oklahoma, and her dad answered the phone. I told him that we would be stopping over and wanted to stop in and say hi. He sounded nervous and asked if we wanted to have dinner. I told him that would be great, and we made our way to their place to have dinner and stay the night. I remember Lina telling me afterward how impressed her mom was with my courage to stop by and see them at their house.

Our connection deepened over time, but it wasn't without challenges. During one call, I mentioned moving away from my parents after marriage. Lina abruptly hung up and ignored my calls for days. When she finally responded, she explained her disapproval of selfishness or abandoning family responsibilities. Her stance only made me admire her more.

I knew I wanted to marry Lina. Proposing wasn't easy; she wanted to finish school first, and I respected that. It took three proposals before she finally said yes, proving persistence pays off. We got engaged and then waited until she was finished with her studies and finally set the date for our wedding on May 18, 1997. The wedding was a traditional Indian wedding, and all of our family and friends attended in Tennessee.

Marrying Lina was the best decision of my life. Her kindness, wisdom, and values have made me a better person. Every day, I feel lucky to share my life with someone so extraordinary. Together, we've built a life full of love, respect, and shared dreams.

"The best love is the kind that awakens the soul and makes us reach for more. It gives us strength to grow and forces us to look at the world in a new way."

-Paulo Coelho

Chapter 6: The Ups and Downs of Being an Entrepreneur

When I was in college, I used to visit my sister's home in Louisville, Colorado, every summer. My sister and brother-in-law had their own t-shirt business and owned t-shirt shops in different malls. I worked in one of these shops, in Boulder, to be exact. Working at a t-shirt shop was really fun. I got to meet new and exciting people all the time and work with my sister. There was an air of creativity in the place, and it always intrigued me.

I remember how it felt to take care of the customers and how satisfying it was when they loved their purchases. I wanted to make the business a success, so I tried to help my sister as much as I could. I would try to work out different ways to market the shop so that traffic would increase and sales would go up. I also worked on making daily operations efficient for the smooth running of the shop.

Over the summers that I worked at the t-shirt shop, I introduced a barcode inventory system to help the store keep track of its inventory. It saved a lot of time and was also cost-effective. It also added the security of complete accuracy, which wouldn't have been possible if the staff had been handling inventory directly. This initiative really helped uplift the business, so I continued to market the business to attract a greater clientele.

This was when I decided that I would venture into the t-shirt industry. The motel business wasn't enough for me. I needed to invest my creativity and ideas in a booming and prosperous business, and this seemed like the perfect idea.

I may sound like a workaholic, but I did more than just work; I also enjoyed my time there and made sure to socialize as much as I could. I made a few friends down there with whom I would go out at night. I did that quite frequently, and many times, I would get back home quite late. Of course, I was a young boy, and my sister was trying to protect me. So, after telling me numerous times to get my act straight, she finally put her foot down. She was really upfront with me and told me that if I wanted to live in her house, I would be her responsibility and would have to follow the rules of the house. Me being the rebellious little angry boy that I was, I couldn't agree to those terms. To me, she was taking away my freedom when I was supposed to be making memories in the summer. So, I told her that I wasn't her kid, and she wasn't my parent, so she had no business schooling me. I immediately left her home to go back to my parent's home in Oklahoma.

Now that I look back at that incident and reflect, I realize that she was doing what any adult would do: protecting me. I realize now that she did a lot for me and that whatever she was doing was because she cared about me. Of course, a young me would've never understood that. But I was grateful for the opportunity to be exposed to her business, which really helped me learn a lot.

I decided to begin my own business venture in Fort Collins. So, I moved there a few months before my fiancé and I were supposed to get married. I believed that Fort Collins would be the perfect place to open up my t-shirt business, which I named The T-shirt Gallery. My goal was to open multiple locations and possibly create my own franchise.

I moved to Fort Collins in March of 1997 and found a small but cozy townhouse to rent. It wasn't anything big or elegant, but it was good enough for Lina and me to begin our new lives. It was a one-bedroom house, and I knew we would be completely comfortable there. Once I was done settling into the new place, it was time for me to start looking for a location for my business. This task turned out to be so much harder than I had thought. I spent weeks trying to find the perfect location, and it proved to be a challenge because I had no contacts in the city. As a workaround, I would go around introducing myself to local commercial real estate agents to try and find someone who could find a suitable spot for me. That's when I met Steve. Steve was a commercial real estate agent, and he was well-connected to the community. He had some great leads for locations for my business.

It was with his help that I was able to find a spectacular spot for my store. It was in downtown Fort Collins, right above a well-known, old-time restaurant called Catacombs Restaurant. Since it was a commercial area, it was perfect for opening up my business there. I soon became friends with the owner of the restaurant, Nico. The landlord of the building was an older gentleman who had owned the building for a long time. He had a plethora of information to share with me, and I was more than happy to learn from him. The t-shirt shop was 1200 square feet, and it had previously been a retail store.

The landlord helped me tremendously with his knowledge and expertise, as I basically had no credit history or knowledge regarding leasing a space. As I moved forward, I realized that there was a lot that I needed to do.

First of all, I needed to come up with funds for my business. I reached out to my close family and friends and requested their assistance by borrowing approximately $30,000 for my business. Luckily for me, I have really supportive friends and family who were able to help me secure these funds quickly. I will be forever grateful to everyone who supported me and helped me start my first venture.

Now that the funds were available, I had to get to work to manage everything within that budget. So, my next step was to involve an attorney and an accountant. I needed their help to understand how to navigate starting my business and signing a lease for the store. It was during this time that I learned the most important lesson about starting a business: you always need a knowledgeable attorney and accountant who specializes in your business. They can help take your business to heights that you couldn't possibly reach yourself.

I met Tim, my attorney, through my real estate agent. And it was Tim who introduced me to Chuck, my accountant. Both of them were great at their jobs and pretty good at helping small businesses start up. I still have the same accounting firm taking care of my personal finances and taxes after all these years, even though I moved from Colorado to Ohio a long time ago.

Once I had signed the lease with my landlord, I had to start the improvements in the shop. But the problem was that I was on a tight budget. I had to take care of the construction, designing, marketing, inventory, equipment, and other miscellaneous costs within the $30,000 budget.

Shondra, one of Lina's friends from college, who was an interior designer, helped me put together my vision for the T-shirt Gallery. The result was a lively, colorful, and brilliant store that would leave anyone walking in mesmerized. Once the design was done, I tried to be creative with the other costs to remain within my budget.

I split my workday into two parts. During the day, I would work on inventory and marketing materials. I would place orders for the shop and create all the marketing content, and at night, I would do the construction myself. This taught me a great lesson in managing my business too. I learned how to interact with city officials to get a permit for construction. For specialized tasks like plumbing, electrical, and mechanical work, I hired subcontractors who worked alongside me to get their work done.

Once the major construction was completed, the only thing left was the winding up, finishing, and setting up of the inventory. I took care of the final touches, which included painting and polishing the store by myself, as I couldn't afford to exceed my budget.

It only took a few months to get all the work done, but by the time the store was ready to be open for business, my wedding was around the corner, and there was no way that I could work at the t-shirt shop during my wedding. So, the next order of business was to hire someone who would take care of the store and drive sales while I was away for my wedding and honeymoon. I knew that this was a big ask, and I needed someone really special for the job.

I put up a few ads looking for someone who would be interested in working as a sales associate. I received many applications and was able to pick a couple of people to start working at the shop. I was especially lucky to find Renee, who was a college student and looked after the store while I was away for the wedding and our honeymoon. She did a great job at the t-shirt store, which is why we remain in touch even now and are still friends.

She is currently married and an attorney in Washington, D.C., and is highly successful, which is nothing less than what I expected of her. She was exceptionally talented and hardworking, even when she worked at my store. She was always really driven and passionate about her work. All those years of working together led us to become friends, which hasn't changed even now.

When Lina and I got back from our honeymoon, I continued working at the t-shirt shop. I worked tirelessly to continue to grow our customer base. One of the techniques was the introduction of screen-printing services. It was then that I learned how to do screen printing by myself, and it was quite a fun experience.

I purchased a four-color press and started doing screen printing for other small businesses and sports teams. Since this was a new service, a lot of sales and marketing techniques were involved in making it a success. And I was so glad that I was able to refer back to the sales and marketing classes I had taken at college. The information that I learned there was quite crucial for me to successfully launch my business and new services.

I hired a few more people to help around the store. Among them was an airbrush artist who did some really cool work. I was so impressed by the work that I had him paint a large canvas mural of The Lion King because that was the movie that Lina and I had watched on our first date. We still have that canvas mural in one of our bedrooms.

I also employed Lina's brother, who came out to stay with us during the summer at the store. It was really fun to have him there and even more fun to get to know him. He was just a 14-year-old boy, but he was really hardworking and came up with some great ideas for the shop. He taught me a lot during his stay with us. This was also another important lesson I learned in life: that we can learn from people of all ages. Just because someone is younger, it doesn't mean they don't have anything valuable to teach us. He helped me come up with so many designs for the printed t-shirts, and it was really fun to be able to bring out our creativity and work on something together.

After a while, my wife started working for an IT company in Longmont, Colorado. It was just about thirty minutes south of Fort Collins, which was an ideal distance for her. She enjoyed that job, but then she got an offer from an even better one. However, this job was in Denver, so we decided to move closer to her job. I continued to commute to Fort Collins every day to work at the t-shirt shop.

We started socializing and making friends. We would go hiking on the weekends. In winter, we learned how to ski so we could go on skiing trips together. It was a wonderful experience to be able to see the mountains every day and enjoy life while we were building and living it.

We never got lost on our way because we always had the vast mountains to guide us. We used to go walking in the Old Town Square and have dinners. Fort Collins was gaining popularity for its microbreweries, so we would occasionally go out there and try some microbrews.

We were also able to visit my sister and her family in Boulder sometimes. Other times, they would come over to our place, and we would all hang out together. It was quite fun to be able to stay in touch with friends and family without having to travel too much.

However, things were too good to last too long, so something traumatic came along.

It was a beautiful sunny day, and I was driving southbound on the interstate at the speed limit. Another car coming northbound lost control and ended up crashing head-on into my car at 65 mph.

"The only thing that is certain in life is that accidents will happen."

-Benjamin Franklin

Chapter 7: Survival of the Fittest

It was one of the most horrifying moments of my life. I was trapped, and I knew I couldn't do anything to save myself. I was driving in the center lane with a semi-truck on my right and another one right behind me. On my left was another car. I could switch lanes or hit the brakes, but that could lead to a worse accident. I tried my best to slow down my car to prevent a collision with the car hurtling towards me. But I had already deduced the crash was inevitable.

Right on impact, my car spun out a few times, leaving me disoriented, and then toppled over into the ditch on the right, where it ended up on its side. I don't remember how I got out of my car or even unbuckled my seatbelt. All I know is that when I got out, people were rushing to my aid. I saw someone bring a blanket for me to lie down, and I remember thinking that was unnecessary. Why would I need a blanket? I told them I was okay, but then someone told me that I was bleeding and needed to lie down. That's when I saw the blood seeping into the blanket I was lying on. I hadn't realized I was injured that badly.

As I lay there, waiting for the ambulance, the people stayed with me. I remember asking one of them whether anyone else was hurt. To my surprise, they told me that no one else had been hurt in the accident. I was the only one who needed medical attention. The other driver, whose car had gone out of control and crashed into mine, was doing fine and was able to walk out of his car unscathed.

Despite my injury, I was happy to hear that no one else was injured. The wait seemed to last for hours when it had been just a few minutes. I was uncomfortable and bleeding, and I had yet to see the damage to my car. Finally, the ambulance arrived, and I was on my way to the hospital.

The ride to the hospital was very bumpy, and it made me even more uncomfortable than I had been on the road. It was my first time in an ambulance, and my experience with it made me swear off being in an ambulance again. I cannot physically be in an ambulance again.

I asked one of the responders to get in touch with Lina. She was at work, and they could easily get a hold of her there. Once they informed her about my accident, she told them she was on her way to the hospital.

At the hospital, the doctors told us that I needed to get stitches in my left ear and staples on the left side of my head. This was because when the car had spun out of control and rolled over multiple times until it fell into the ditch, I had hit the driver's side window with my head multiple times, which led to the glass being shattered.

Small fragments of glass were still lodged in my head. According to the doctor, this is why I didn't remember getting out of the car. I had a concussion. The shattered glass pieces in my head eventually fell out over the next couple of days.

Once I was doing better and started healing, Lina and I went to the salvage yard to retrieve some of my belongings from the car. When we saw the state of the car, we were both shocked beyond belief. The car was a complete wreck. It was unimaginable that anyone would have made it out alive of that car. It was truly a miracle that I had survived the crash.

I discovered later that my VW Jetta had a rollover bar that saved me from becoming meat pulp. Without that feature, I probably would've died that day.

When the accident occurred, we were living in an apartment in Aurora, Colorado, and had a few friends living in the same apartment complex as us. We also had friends living in our neighboring suburbs. Being so close to my friends and having such a big group of friends and acquaintances around me meant that we could have a great social life.

We all shared the same interests and loved doing the same activities, so we were able to hang out and do things together all the time. Sometimes, we would go skiing on the weekends. Other times, we would just hang out at each other's places and have a movie or game night. If nothing, we would all go out for burgers and drinks at our convenience.

The great thing about all my friends was that we were all in similar life phases. We were all recently married or were getting married and trying to build a life individually and as couples. We all were starting new lives and were full of hope and excitement for the future.

Lina was doing a wonderful job at her workplace, and she was really happy working there. She worked at Anderson Consulting, which was part of Arthur Anderson. Soon after she started working there, the company split off from Arthur Anderson and rebranded as Accenture.

Since this was an international company, Lina could travel all around the world. She had multiple clients and companies across the globe that she was able to consult. This meant that she had a very hectic schedule and was traveling frequently.

Lina would leave every week on Monday and return on Thursday evenings. Honestly, it wasn't easy to be apart for so long each week. I dreaded Mondays more because it meant that Lina wouldn't be home for a couple of days. It was tough to be apart, but we had to build our futures, so we didn't let our emotions dictate our lives. The time apart allowed us to focus on our work and ourselves and give our all to our careers.

After my car accident, Lina and I mutually decided to sell the shop. We both agreed that it was dangerous for me to be driving every day for an hour and a half from Aurora to Fort Collins for work. I may have survived this accident, but we didn't want to risk another one.

This was my first time selling a business. I had no idea where to begin and how to evaluate the market value of my business. So, I reached out to a few contacts that I had made over the past year. I asked for their advice on how I could go about selling my business without incurring a loss. It was all uncharted territory for me, and I could use all the help I got.

I reached out to my real estate agent, Steve, as well. He suggested that I speak with a business broker. These are professionals who specialize in helping people buy and sell businesses. That's how I got in touch with James at a business brokerage company. He told me that he had several businesses for sale in Colorado and had a stream of people lined up to purchase businesses.

The first step was to evaluate the business and come up with a sale price. This was important because we had to set a price that would bring me profit, but we also couldn't make it exorbitantly high. Once the price was settled, we could move on to marketing the business for sale.

During this process, I discovered that it was much harder to sell a leased space than a location you own. Despite the hurdles, James came up with a price for the business. After commissions were paid, I would end up essentially breaking even and would get the initial money I borrowed from family and friends and be able to pay them back.

We found a buyer for the business, and after about 45 days of him evaluating the business and getting his financing in place, we were able to close the deal on the t-shirt shop. After closing the shop, we paid the money back to all of the family and friends that I had borrowed from to get the store started. That's how my t-shirt business came to an end.

I started applying for some jobs and ended up as a Department Manager at Mervyn's Department store in Aurora. It was close to our apartment, so that was good for me. While I was at Mervyn's, I met several people who worked there, and we became friends outside of the workplace. We stay in touch to this day.

One of my good friends from Denver also started working there in security, and we would sometimes end up having lunch together when we were working the same shifts. I learned a lot about how corporate business works and realized some of the major differences between corporate and small businesses.

One of the major things working for a corporation is the amount of support you have from the multiple departments within the corporate structure. They had everything from legal to human resources to training and much more. As a small business owner, you had to wear multiple hats.

I realized there were some hats I didn't even know existed until working at Mervyn's. I have been asked by many people if I regret starting The T-Shirt Gallery, and I always have the same answer: No. I don't have any regrets because all the lessons that I learned during this period in my life were so valuable. As an entrepreneur, there will be challenges every day, but how you handle them and move forward determines your success.

I learned all about starting a business, what paperwork needs to be completed, how to get loans, how to get a leased space, working with contractors, working with banks, working with other local businesses, how to sell a business, and the importance of hiring the best attorney and accountant. Even today, I give this advice to everyone who asks me about starting a new business venture. The first thing you should do is hire the best attorney and accountant for your industry or business.

"The survival of the fittest is not the strongest or the fastest who survive. It is the one who is most adaptable to change."

-Charles Darwin

Chapter 8: Back to My Roots

I was always looking at different businesses, trying to figure out what my next venture would be. My sister introduced me to several people, most of whom were in the hotel industry. I was rather impressed by the way they were running their businesses. I had hardly been exposed to businesses working on such a high level; the most I had witnessed were smaller motel operations. So, watching these people conduct their large-scale hotel businesses really opened my eyes.

Everyone I knew in Oklahoma had small motels, and some of the people I met in Colorado were operating a franchise hotel with at least 60 rooms or more. This was great exposure for me as it brought me up to speed with the business infrastructure in the area and allowed me to widen my horizons and explore things that I had never thought to explore before.

These operations gave me the idea of the possibility of being in the hospitality industry, but not the way I had learned to be. My parents owned a motel, but I wanted to do more than that. I wanted to have a proper, high-end hotel with lavish rooms and services.

That's when I got into a discussion with a college friend from Oklahoma. We talked about the possibility of buying or building our own hotel in Colorado. I knew that the hotel industry was doing well because tourism was flourishing, and there was an influx of business travelers in the state. So, I began my research on how hotels were doing in my area.

My research led me to a wonderful discovery. While there were various motels and hotels in the area, there was still a need for more, especially those that were franchised and independent. That was the green signal I needed.

I began searching for a suitable location for my hotel and found one in Castle Rock, just 20 minutes South of Denver. This was an up-and-coming area, which meant there was a need for developmental projects, and building my hotel here would make me a pioneer in the area. I would have less competition and a substantial population to supply to.

New outlet malls had been built there. The Castle Pines Golf Course was also there, designed by Jack Nicklaus. Both these businesses brought many people into the area for travel and recreational activity.

My first order of business was to look at my competitors and analyze how I could set myself and my hotel apart from them. There were only a few hotels in the area, so I knew it wouldn't be too hard for me to outdo myself and create an experience unlike any other in the area.

However, I also knew it would be difficult to become a franchisee for big brand hotels such as Marriott, Hilton, or IHG. So, I decided to go for a brand that would be easily accessible to me. I went to Wyndham – known as Cendant then –as many other Indian owners were going to Cendant to become franchisees.

I met with Steve from Cendant and discussed the area. I proposed my idea of constructing a Days Inn & Suites and how it would be a great addition to the area. I asked him to guide me through the process, and he told me that I had to submit an application for my hotel idea, but it would be better if I had control of the site since that would increase the chances of approval.

So, I embarked on my journey to look for suitable sites. I drove around and found a few sites. Then, I found the realtors' contact information and called up a few of them.

One particular site was up on a hill, and you could see Interstate 25 from there. I felt that it would be the perfect site for my hotel as it was clearly visible from afar, so anyone coming through Interstate 25 could see it, and it was also easily accessible, which would definitely lead to more traffic.

This was also the exit where the outlet malls and one of the main exits to get to the Castle Pines Golf Course were located. So, any traffic coming to these businesses could be easily diverted to the hotel.

I called the agent for that particular site and signed a contract for the land so I could begin my application process for the hotel. I proceeded with my application for the Days Inn & Suites, a 64-room, three-story interior corridor property with a pool.

While the application was in process, I contacted some banks and learned how to get financing for my business.

That's when I came to know more about putting together a formal business plan. I also learned how to create a development budget and a proforma with five-year projections.

I had a meeting with a lender from a small bank and presented my vision for the hotel to him. He loved the idea. As we continued to review the plan and discuss the project, we became good friends, and I learned a lot from him.

He liked the project and decided to present it to his board. With a little bit of effort, the board approved the project. The total project was $3 million, so we had to come up with at least $600,000 for our equity. I was already in discussion with a friend of mine from Oklahoma and another one from Denver, and we had collectively decided that the four of us would be equal partners.

The three of them had their share of capital already, but I didn't. I had to ask my family and friends to let me borrow the money to make the cut for equity. I made a bunch of phone calls and was surprisingly able to put together the money rather quickly.

I was in charge of putting the agreements together and doing all the accounting, even though I had no previous experience or knowledge in the field. I did get a generic Limited Liability Company template and put together the agreement. However, I knew I couldn't do the accounting, so I asked my partners if one of them could handle accounting as it really wasn't my forte.

They told me that I could use QuickBooks, and it would make the process smooth for me. They said that I would be able to figure it out quickly. However, that turned out to be a huge mistake, as you will soon find out.

I reached out to a few friends in Denver to help me find a general contractor. Fortunately, I was able to find one without wasting too much time, and I hired him.

We were now getting quite close to starting our project. I knew I would be overlooking construction, so I needed to be well-equipped. I went to a bookstore and bought expert-level books on general construction, how to read blueprints, and understanding construction lingo.

I vividly remember the day I was sitting with a buddy in a coffee shop and sketching the layout of the hotel that I had envisioned. The three-story hotel with an indoor pool had a golf theme to make it a unique experience for the guests. I decided to name the suites "par suites." We also had a few jacuzzi suites that I decided to name "hole-in-one suites." We planned to add a putter and a putting green in each of these suites.

I found a few places where I could buy different golf memorabilia so that we would have a golf theme throughout the hotel. We started construction in October of 1999, and the hotel opened in April of 2000. I was quite satisfied since the hotel had been built and inaugurated on time without going out of budget. We were right on track. It was even more impressive because this was my first developmental project, and we worked through the winter to finish it on time.

I would wake up every morning and be at the site at 6 am. I would stay until 5 or 6 in the evening, and I was always dressed appropriately in my construction gear to fit right in with the crew that was actually doing the construction. A few times, I went in and scraped ice and shoveled snow to ensure we didn't slow down and get behind. I also started networking while I was on the job site and got to know several businesses in the area, including the golf pro at Castle Pines Golf Course.

Rockyard Brewery was just within walking distance of the hotel, and I became good friends with the brewery's owner. We decided that it would be a great idea to help each other out. So, I proposed to him that I could give wooden tokens to the guests at my hotel for one free beer at his brewery. It was very unlikely they would have just one beer; they would probably end up buying more. They might also order food with their free beer, which would mean additional revenue and more traffic for his business. And it wouldn't hurt me either to give my guests a free amenity.

Expectedly, the owner was a little hesitant at first, but then I told him to keep all the tokens for each month and total them, and if he didn't make enough money from the customers, I would pay him for the cost of those beers. He was sold on that.

After the first month, he asked me to keep giving out the tokens as it was reaping great returns for his business. My business was starting to ramp up, too, and we were getting busier by the month. I was struggling with accounting, though, and didn't have a stronghold over how to enter the information, which resulted in the books being really sloppy.

Lina, my wife, was still traveling for work and was gone most of the weekdays. Sometimes, I would travel to her; her company would either pay for her to fly home or for me to go see her.

When she did come home, we would play golf, go hiking, or just hang out with friends. We also learned how to ski. It was all really nice.

When Lina wasn't home, I would keep myself busy with work. I would perform my managerial duties as well as work one shift in the morning and do the paperwork, hiring, training, and other trivial things around the hotel.

There had been a few occasions when someone would call off, and I would have to do a double shift, clean rooms, and do maintenance. I learned a lot about dealing with all types of people from an employee/employer standpoint and dealing with difficult situations.

There was one incident that was very disturbing. I had hired a night auditor; he had worked at another big corporate-owned hotel. When he came to our hotel, I was impressed with his resume. As I learned more about him, I discovered that his dad was an influential personality in Castle Rock and felt he would be a great addition to our hotel.

There was a weekend when I went to visit Lina, and when I got back, I noticed that the bank balance was low and checked the deposits coming in from both cash deposits as well as credit cards. I noticed that the credit card deposits didn't come in for several days and called the merchant services to investigate.

They told me that someone had refunded the full amount for several nights, which would have been deposited into our account. I told them that it had to be a mistake, but they told me that the full amount of the deposit was refunded to a single credit card before closing the batch each night.

They couldn't disclose the name on the card but gave me the last four digits. I used that information, and through some investigation, I was able to find the culprit; it was our night auditor. He had been doing this for several nights a week, and the total amount came to over ten thousand dollars.

I contacted the bank, spoke with the branch manager, and asked if he would be able to help me recover the lost money. Luckily for me and my business, he was able to help me out. Shortly after, I had the police brought in, and the night auditor was arrested.

I followed up with his previous employer and alerted them about what he had done at our hotel. They did some investigation of their own and found out that he had done the same at their hotel, but the total amount was worth hundreds of thousands of dollars over several years. They hadn't been able to catch it because he had been quite clever in his ways.

There were a few other adventures and mishaps as well, and it was definitely a 24-hour business, which reminded me so much of my childhood when my parents would always be at the motel worrying about something related to their business. About one and a half years into this, I did multiple shifts and housekeeping, about 72 hours straight, and eventually got exhausted. The bookkeeping was a mess, and my partners were asking me what was going on. I explained that I was doing the best I could, but I couldn't handle it all on my own—I needed to hire a manager.

"There are only two lasting bequests we can hope to give our children. One of these is roots, the other, wings."

-Hodding Carter

Chapter 9: The Way Out, Moving to Cincinnati

The others didn't like the idea. One of my business partners decided to move to Colorado and run the property himself. I was given a few weeks to pack my stuff and move out. Lina and I decided to start looking for places where we could move. We stayed at a close friend's house in Denver while we were figuring out our next move.

We went to Connecticut, where my wife's project was, and looked around for a place. But we didn't find anything suitable. Then, we went to Atlanta and searched for a place to settle down, but nothing popped out to us in either of those areas. We went to Cincinnati because my brother lived there, and after looking around for a while, we decided that it might be the best location to move to, considering I had to find a job and Lina's family was in Tennessee. Moving here would mean that we would be closer to both families.

Shortly after arriving in Cincinnati, I received a fax from my partners in Colorado for a capital call. They told me that the property wasn't doing so well and that I had left the bookkeeping a mess. They couldn't figure out what was going on. I didn't have any money to offer, so the only option was to have my shares diluted.

Both Lina and I were devastated. I was still searching for a job. It was a blessing that Lina still had her job so she could support us while I looked for one. Thankfully, we were staying with my brother, so we didn't have to pay rent.

As soon as I got settled into his place, I started looking for a job. I applied to a lot of places and landed several interviews. I remember how tough it was, but somehow, I was able to secure a position at a car dealership in the northern part of Cincinnati. I got the paperwork done and started training immediately.

This was a commission-based job with a two-week training program. I wasn't a fan of commission-based jobs, but I needed a source of income, and this was it. After a few days of training, the job just didn't feel right for me. I wasn't satisfied trying to sell people cars whether they needed them or not and always trying to upsell them into something they may not need at all.

I struggled with this feeling for a while until I decided to quit and find something else to do. As I continued searching for a job, I received another fax from my partners at the hotel. It was another capital call request. Again, I did not have any money and couldn't borrow any more from anyone, so I called my attorney and asked his advice. He told me that the best thing to do was to just let them dilute me and get out of the partnership altogether.

This was a tough decision as I was still guaranteeing the loan, and I did not know if the lender would let my name come off the loan guarantee. I called the lender and explained the entire situation to him. He said he would see if he could do anything to help me out. A few days later, he called and told me that he had a meeting with the bank board and explained my situation, and they agreed to take my name off the guarantee. In all that chaos, it was such a relief.

If I hadn't made that phone call that day, I don't think I could have just walked away by diluting myself out of the partnership. Even with the lender removing my name as a guarantor, it was still a tough spot to be in because I now had a debt of $150,000 and had to pay all that money back to all my friends and family who had believed in me and backed me up.

I had my attorney send a letter to the partners letting them know that I would not be able to put any additional money into the hotel and that I relinquish my shares to them. This was the end of my days as a hotelier.

This venture taught me so much about business. I should not have created my partnership agreement from a template and would have been better off if I had had an attorney create the agreement. This is what lawyers do every day as professionals; they help you make agreements in a way that would protect everyone in case of any trouble. I should have asked people who had been in the hotel business about how to structure deals and agreements. I should have taken advice about other best practices.

The problem was that I had a chip on my shoulder at the time because I was young and thought I knew everything because I was able to get the land, the franchise, secure financing, and build the hotel. My ego got the best of me, and I thought I was the smartest guy in the room.

Today, I tell people all the time that I am not the smartest guy in the room, and I don't want to be. I need to surround myself with people who are smarter and more experienced than me so they can guide me and help me move more clearly.

As I continued to look for a job, I ended up learning about a vacancy for a general manager of Bally Total Fitness. I thought it would be great to work in the fitness industry, so I applied there. I got a call for the interview and was offered the position, but there was a catch: I would have to go to Indianapolis for training for a month, and then I would start as a general manager in Dayton and then eventually move to a Cincinnati location.

I was super excited for this job. Lina was still traveling for work and continuing to grow her career, with lots of experience with different clients. When I first got to Indianapolis, I stayed at a hotel, got to the fitness club, and reported for duty.

When the training started, I was learning about how the fitness industry worked, and I started to work out and get in shape. After a month of training, I moved to the Dayton Club and became the general manager. I was staying at a hotel near the club and would work from 8 am to close every day and some weekends as well.

It was a small club, and I was able to connect with some of the members, help them with their issues, understand their needs, and start to make small but significant changes in helping deliver the best customer service possible. We eventually started getting more members and were also retaining the current ones.

Within three weeks, they asked me to move to the Blue Ash club as it was having some difficulty. Once I reached there, I met the staff and introduced myself to everyone. I met so many people there who would later become my best friends as well as business partners.

I met one of my area directors, Kirk, and we became really good friends. Along with him, I met Mike and Jed, with whom I became good friends within a short amount of time. I didn't have a lot of friends previously, so it was nice to have some friends to hang out with outside of work.

Mike was a sales agent and was very young. It was interesting how great he was at connecting with people of all ages. I learned a lot from Mike while he was working at the Blue Ash club, and then they transferred him to another club within six months, but we still stayed in touch and remained friends.

Jed was the Operations Manager at the club, and he did a fantastic job of keeping the operations running smoothly. He was a great personal trainer himself. Jed would spend hours training me, and I got in the best shape of my life. He also provided personal training for Lina.

One day, while I was working, a guy named Craig walked into the club and asked about getting a job as a personal trainer, so the front desk gave me his resume. I sat down with Craig as his resume was amazing, and I wanted to know more about him. We spent about an hour talking, and I discovered so much about him and hired him on the spot.

As the months went by, Craig and I would sit together after hours, have coffee, and get to know each other. He asked me a few times what I was doing there, and I told him I was still trying to figure out what I wanted to do when I grew up. As I learned more about Craig, I discovered that he had a vast amount of experience in real estate and was also an adjunct instructor at a local college that offered various real estate and investment courses.

Craig became my mentor, and I thought to myself it would have been great to have Craig as a mentor when I was younger and just starting out. The importance of a mentor is significant. Whenever anyone asks me for advice on how to improve their personal or professional life, I tell them to get a mentor. Just ask someone whom you look up to. The worst-case scenario is that they say no, but at least you'd have given it a shot.

Around the same time, Lina and I found out we were expecting our first child, and it was all really exciting. As her due date was getting closer, we decided to buy our first house in Mason, Ohio, and make it our home. Right before we moved into our house, I decided to take three months off as paternity leave and explore the possibility of venturing into home inspections because Craig had told me about the home inspection industry and how it was a flourishing market with great potential.

"Life is what happens when you're busy making other plans."

- John Lennon

Chapter 10: Once More!

At first, when Craig and I talked about home inspections. I didn't know what home inspections were as I had never lived in a house; I had always stayed in a hotel or rented an apartment. Craig described what is involved in a home inspection, and I found it fascinating and exciting.

It goes something like this – you go into a different house, learn about different people, and interact with them to teach them about the potential defects and the maintenance of a house. The best part of this type of work is that every house is different, and therefore it never gets boring.

Craig had a wealth of knowledge about home inspection, and he was quite motivating and inspiring. He gave me some cassette tapes of Tony Robbins – Personal Power. This was the first time I had heard of Tony Robbins, and it was great listening to him every day. With each passing day, I understood why Craig liked listening to Tony. Now, I listen to him occasionally and have also had the opportunity to attend Tony's live seminars.

Craig used to teach the home inspection classes himself, but he advised me to go to Columbus to take the two-week class so I get an objective perspective. I decided to do that and enrolled in the class. I stayed for two weeks in Columbus and went through the class. There were about 20 people in the class, all from different backgrounds.

The instructor owned his own inspection company in Columbus, and it was a franchise. The parent company had over 200 locations across the country. He had been in the business for years and had about ten inspectors, two office staff, and an office; it was a real business.

During the class, I would always listen carefully and soak in everything that I was taught in those two weeks. I wanted to learn everything about the process of doing home inspections.

I believe it helped that I had previously been involved in real estate and construction. After each session, I would talk to the instructor, and he would tell me more about the business and how I could potentially come work for him at his franchised home inspection company.

This was intriguing, and I thought it would be a great opportunity for me to learn more about the business and the inspection industry. During the last few days of the class, I decided to ask him if I could come to work for him, and he agreed. I would have to come up to Columbus and do the inspections in that area as he did not have a location in Cincinnati. However, he did express that I could potentially buy the Cincinnati franchise territory at some point down the road once I had more experience. I drove up every week and stayed with a friend at their hotel. I would go out and do inspections during the day and then write the reports in the evening. It was tough as I would be away from Lina and our newborn daughter, Dharma.

Thank goodness that my parents had come to stay with Lina to help out with Dharma. It was comforting to know that we had the support needed between Lina going back to work and me being gone to learn about the inspection industry.

I went out for about two weeks with Paul, one of the senior inspectors who had been doing inspections for almost ten years. He was a wealth of knowledge, and I learned so much from him about how to do inspections, how to interact with clients, and how to write reports and deliver them to clients. There were a lot of things that I learned about the process of getting the inspection order, preparing the information for the inspection, and how to interact with clients. After two weeks of training, the owner decided I was knowledgeable enough to go out and do the inspection myself.

I didn't think that was enough training, but I was also new to the industry, and the owner had been doing this for many years now, so I went out as he would schedule me for inspections and started performing inspections all on my own.

It was scary at the beginning because I would run into things that I wasn't sure about. I would call Paul during the inspection and ask him about what I was seeing and how I should report them.

The report writing was another tough area for me to grasp as it was all done on a paper document, and then after the inspection was complete, I would go back and use the report writing software and type up the report. We were taking pictures with a digital camera but would print the pictures and add them to the report that was generated. Then, we would email the report, and, in some cases, we would print and mail the report. I started exploring some other software that was available for the inspection industry and found that there were other software companies that would allow the report to be written and pictures added within the appropriate sections, and then the report could be sent as a PDF via email to the client.

I took some of my findings a few months into working with the owner and discussed how some of these things could be improved. He wasn't big on my ideas and said the way he was doing things was working well, and he had grown his business and wasn't looking to change things.

This was frustrating for me, and within three months of working for him, I decided to give my two weeks' notice and start my own inspection company in Cincinnati.

I needed about $5,000 to get the company started. I reached out to some of the friends and family who had helped me with my previous ventures, and they all said that maybe I should just get a job and not try another new business.

That wasn't going to work for me. I had to follow my passion, and with a strategic plan and a mentor, I decided to borrow the money on a credit card and get the company started. Craig and I cofounded 1st Ohio Inspection Services in 2003. I set up a simple website, and we started marketing to realtors by going to their offices and dropping off rack cards, gift certificates, pens, and candy in hopes of getting them to allow us to do some inspections for their buyers or sellers. I didn't have a physical office, and the house was tough to work from with my parents and a newborn at home, so I would go to FedEx and work from the computer desks they had for customers. I'd use the space to create marketing materials and make phone calls to realtors to schedule in-office presentations about our services.

I decided to use inspection software for reporting and set up different trial accounts to learn about the differences between them and find the one I thought would give my clients the best report. After reviewing the different software providers, I landed on Home Gauge.

It was a great software that allowed the use of digital photographs and the ability to upload the reports on the web, and then the customers could view the report as well as download the report if they needed. I put in a call to the folks at Home Gauge and spoke with the two owners, Russell and Sean.

Russell used to be a home inspector, and Sean was a programmer. They met during a home inspection and decided to create one of the best software for the home inspection industry. I have to say it is one of the best, and we still use it for all of our franchisees.

One of the first homes I inspected was a referral from Mike, whom I had met at Bally's when he was a client there during my time as a GM. We had become friends, and he was starting his career in real estate as an agent. He gave my information to one of his clients. After I had completed the first inspection, it was an amazing feeling to know that I had just done my first inspection and satisfied the customer. I took a little bit longer and really worked on giving the buyers a full and thorough evaluation of the house.

I asked them what profession they were in, what their concerns were, and who was going to live there. These were the things that mattered to me for me to do the best job I could as an inspector.

As I did this over and over, it became clearer that this was going to be something that really separated our company from our competitors. This is also what led me to come up with our tagline for the company: **"Not your ordinary inspection company."**

We were not simply doing an inspection and handing over a report; we were learning about our clients, understanding what they did, and what their concerns were about the home that they were going to buy. One of the key things I learned during the start of my business was to research as much as possible. Every free moment I had was spent reading up and networking with real estate agents and learning about the client's needs.

Evaluating multiple software companies and other vendors was crucial to my success. Doing things on a shoestring budget was crucial as most startups don't require a lot of capital but creativity and thinking outside the box.

"The difference between a successful person and others is not a lack of strength, not a lack of knowledge, but rather a lack of will."

-Vince Lombardi

Chapter 11: The Business Goes On

I was out every day for hours, visiting multiple offices for marketing and getting to know the office managers and some of the agents. I was able to convince a few of them to allow me to present to their new agents, "Home Inspection Defined and Top 10 Defects" to help them as they were taking buyers and sellers through showings.

This was a great opportunity as I was able to show the agents what we do and how we work as professionals. We were an asset to them and not a hurdle. I learned that most agents did not like home inspectors because they would "kill the deal" by scaring clients with words or phrases that were not necessary.

I would always discuss the property with the client in detail, whether they were buying or selling. I would also mention the condition of the home at the time of the inspection and how to keep the house maintained. Then, I would make recommendations based on what I discovered about the property.

It also helped to keep their professions in mind and tailor the conversation based on their knowledge of how things functioned so they wouldn't get scared. It simply helped them become aware of the condition of the property. My job was to educate my clients about their properties, not to present my opinion.

When I started the business, I didn't have an office, so I didn't have an office number either. I used my cell phone number on all marketing materials, business cards, and my website. This was a huge mistake, but I didn't know any better back then. I still get phone calls on my personal number from clients wanting to schedule a home inspection.

It doesn't bother me at all. I did put in a lot of effort to get my name out there, and one of the things that worked out in my favor was putting up a discount on my services. There was a time when I printed out flyers for home and termite inspections for only $200. That was a heavily discounted price, as most people were charging around $350.

It wasn't long before my efforts came to fruition. I started getting calls and scheduling inspections. I was doing two to three inspections almost every day.

I made notes about the client to determine the kind of inspection they would need. I would do my review, which was then followed by scheduling the inspection. It was a tedious process, but it didn't take long to get the hang of it.

After I was done with my inspection, I would write the reports. These reports were sent to the client and their real estate agent. Many a time, I found myself working up until midnight writing these reports. And then, the next day, I would be back to doing inspections at the break of dawn.

It was tough, but it was the path I had chosen for myself. I had to get things done. Over the next few months, I tried to come home early and spend more time with my family. No matter how busy I was, I didn't want to miss out on precious memories. I wanted to watch my daughter grow up and spend time with my wife whenever I could.

I would work on reports when Dharma would take a nap. When she would go to sleep, Lina and I would spend some time together and catch up on how things were going.

Eventually, life got busier for me, but luckily, Craig was always there to assist me. He helped find a few good gentlemen who were interested in doing inspections.

Tom and Kevin both came on as inspectors, and I started working with them to learn the way we did our inspections and the report writing software. They were both quick learners and quite personable. I knew they would fit right in with our way of doing inspections and conducting ourselves as professionals.

Four months into the business, I met with a mortgage company owner. It was a large company that wanted to include a home and termite inspection with every mortgage. The home buyers wouldn't have to pay immediately for the inspection as the mortgage company would be paying us.

It was a great business deal, but there was a catch; we had to do the inspections for a discount. Since we were guaranteed payment by the mortgage company every month, we decided it was a good partnership. It sent more business our way and gave us more exposure in the Cincinnati real estate market. Our hands were full.

While I was doing the marketing and scheduling, Tom and Kevin would go to houses and do the inspections.

We started doing commercial inspections, termite inspections, and radon testing. There were so many auxiliary types of inspections that it became hard for me to choose one. I invested my time in learning all about them. I even took a few classes that provided certifications so I could prove my eligibility for the work.

Besides commercial inspections, I also did relocation inspections when I was in Columbus. I did a little bit of research on the internet and reached out to a few companies I found online.

I went through their application process and got approved to be a preferred vendor in the Cincinnati area. They were quite impressed by our work and quick turnaround time.

That led me to sublease an office space from the mortgage company. It was really exciting to finally have an office and not conduct my business from FedEx Kinko's.

Once we had an office, it became easier to sort things out. We needed an additional hand at the business, and we found just the perfect candidate for that. Craig's daughter, Christy, was looking for a job for the summer, so she came in and helped out with administrative duties. She was great at what she did – she would get things done quickly and efficiently. I'd say she helped me organize my business.

On the other hand, Lina was back to work with Accenture and traveling to Columbus for her client. It was a relief that my parents were still with us and helping with Dharma. I wouldn't have been able to do it alone.

One busy day, Craig and I were sitting down and having coffee when he told me he wanted to renounce his ownership of the company.

I was shocked and asked, "Did I do something wrong?"

He told me that I was the one doing all the work, going out every day, and exerting myself just to make something out of the business. He was just guiding me and, \therefore, didn't believe he should have ownership. I didn't feel that was right, and I told him I didn't know how I would ever pay him back.

He said, "Pay it forward. Help someone else that might need the help."

That stopped me. I couldn't think of anything else at that moment. I couldn't believe this was happening.

He reassured me that I was doing the work and he was just guiding me, so it was only fair that I was the sole owner. I told Lina everything Craig had said, and she couldn't believe it either. We both knew Craig well, but we couldn't figure out *why* he would do that. The only thing that made sense was how genuine he was and how he truly meant everything he said.

Craig and I continued meeting regularly. He would still mentor me. He could tell that I still had some weight on my shoulders and asked me if I had ever gotten past the hotel partnership debacle that happened. I told him that it was hard to let go. That's when he advised me to at least make a call to each of my previous partners and let them know whatever happened was in the past.

I did some thinking and then made the phone calls. I have to say it felt like a heavy weight had been lifted off my shoulders. It wasn't a lengthy conversation with any of them, but I told each one of them that what happened was in the past and that I was okay and moving forward. There were no explanations, no further discussions about what had happened, just a simple conversation.

Life was already getting better. That's when I realized that you truly have to put the past behind you to live in the present and be able to look forward to the future.

In January of 2004, Lina and I found out that she was pregnant and we were going to have another baby. We were both so excited! Things were getting busier for the company and the family. July came sooner than expected, and we were just a month away from welcoming our second baby into our lives.

Lina was still working, and I was out doing inspections and marketing and continuing with the company's growth. We were probably doing around 15 inspections a week. I was doing a few more to help out so the guys didn't get overworked.

I still vividly remember the unforgettable inspection in Fairfield, Ohio, in August. I was at a house with a potential buyer. I went up on the roof to check it out. The house had an upper roof, and I decided to move the ladder to the lower roof and climb up so that I could get a good view of the upper roof. I made it up and inspected the roof. Once I was done with that area, I started climbing down the ladder, and all of a sudden, the ladder slipped. The next thing I knew, I was lying on the concrete driveway.

As I got up and looked at my right arm, I saw that it was bleeding. A moment later, I noticed a piece of bone sticking out. My head spun as I applied some pressure with my left hand. The adrenaline kept me going without feeling any pain for a moment.

I asked the potential buyer to call 911, and within five minutes, the ambulance arrived. They had me lay down on the stretcher. The pain started to kick in as the adrenaline began to wear off. It was unbearable, unlike any pain I had experienced before. I asked the EMT if they could get my phone and call Craig so I could let him know what happened and tell him to get ahold of Lina and let her know.

I didn't want her to worry as she was just a few weeks from delivering our second baby. Once I had talked to Craig, I asked the EMT to call Kevin, and when he answered, I said, "Kevin, I just fell off the roof and am on the way to the hospital."

He laughed and told me to stop joking around.

I always like to joke around and have fun, so it wasn't a surprise that he thought I was joking. I gave him the address of the house I was inspecting and asked him to go there and finish the inspection, gather all of my tools, and get my car.

He took care of everything right away. He even finished the report and delivered it to the client and the agent.

While heading to the hospital, which was thankfully only ten minutes away, I asked the EMT for some painkillers. They said they couldn't give me anything until they got me admitted.

Once admitted, they gave me some painkillers. When I woke up, Lina was there. She told me they had done surgery on me, but I would need more surgeries. They couldn't do them all at once as it would be too much for my body to handle.

The doctors came in and told us that I had a compound fracture. Besides that, all the bones in my wrist looked like shattered glass, the elbow had multiple areas of damage, and the bones in my forearm were broken. They warned of compartment syndrome and said they were going to have two sides of my forearm cut open so that it wouldn't swell and cause nerve damage.

I clearly remember the conversation Lina and Craig were having in the hospital room. They were talking about shutting the business down. I spoke up and said that we were not going to shut the business down.

They thought it was the medication talking and told me not to worry about anything. It was a lot for me to take in.

I was discharged from the hospital and got home on the 13th of August in the evening. On the 14th, Lina woke up as she went into labor.

My parents took us to the hospital, and my brother and sister-in-law came to help out. In the hospital room, Lina was in one bed, and they rolled in another bed for me to lay on as I had an external fixator on my arm to keep everything stable.

Lina is truly a blessing in my life. She didn't only take care of me with my given condition but also delivered our second baby within a few hours. We named her Saiya.

Since Lina didn't want to spend another day in the hospital, we left the hospital the same day. After we got home, I spent the next few months sleeping on the couch as I couldn't sleep on a bed with the external fixator. I continued to operate the business by taking phone calls and scheduling the inspections.

Kevin and Tom continued to do the inspections and helped me keep the business running. Craig helped me out during the first year of business as I went through a total of nine surgeries on my arm. It was a tough period, but I was alive, and the business continued to grow.

Many people ask me if I ever regret falling off the roof. I tell them that everything happens for a reason. If we look for the positive in any situation, we can find a way to make it through and come out stronger on the other side.

If I had never fallen off that roof and had continued doing the inspections myself, I would have continued working "in the business" and not "on the business."

"Everything that happens to you is a gift, even if it doesn't feel like it at the time."

- Pema Chodron

Chapter 12: Starting a Franchise Company

A friend of mine, Ajay, who used to live in Cincinnati, moved to North Carolina and got a job at a reputable company. However, he became interested in starting his own home inspection business, just like me, and reached out for advice. I spent several weeks teaching him about the industry and provided him with useful information. Ajay then asked if I could help him set up his business as a licensee of our company, which instantly sparked the idea of franchising. We renamed the business 1st Inspection Services and began offering inspection services to people in North Carolina and Ohio.

During my visit to North Carolina, I spent a week with Ajay. I assisted him in setting up his computer and shared my extensive knowledge of marketing and scheduling. Ajay started his business, and I was pleased to witness his progress.

As a result, several inspectors reached out to me about working at our Cincinnati location. We promptly began performing inspections in Dayton.

Paul, who used to work with me in Columbus when I first entered the home inspection industry, was the first inspector to join us. I remembered him as a skilled inspector who would be an excellent addition to our company. Since Paul was based in Dayton, we expanded our services to that area.

We kept ourselves busy attending to our client's needs, always striving to provide the best services possible. Paul even went above and beyond by conducting presentations for realtors. His caring demeanor and extensive experience made him a hit with everyone. It was a great moment when we received a call from Carl, an old colleague from Columbus who was now working in Dayton. With his arrival, we now had a second inspector in Dayton to help us continue to serve our clients with excellence.

Our company was thriving with the addition of four inspectors, establishing a solid reputation in both Cincinnati and Dayton. Then came John, an experienced inspector from Columbus. He reached out to us regarding job opportunities, and with his vast knowledge, he proved to be an invaluable asset, providing insights beyond inspections. As our business continued to expand, I also contributed to inspections, especially for commercial properties, leveraging my prior experience building hotels and taking courses on commercial property condition assessments.

Around the same time, a friend of my wife's reached out to us about her brother, Harish, who expressed interest in joining the inspection business. After speaking with him for several hours, I was confident that he would make an excellent franchisee. We promptly got him started, and he soon hit the ground running in New Jersey.

After starting my business, I received great support from Nick, the founder of InterNACHI. He assisted me in various aspects of the business and even invited us to have a booth at a national conference in Canada in 2005. This was a wonderful opportunity to promote our franchise and educate our inspectors. It was our first time exhibiting at an international conference, and we were thrilled.

Following the conference, a gentleman from Ocala, Florida, expressed interest in buying the entire territory of Florida as a master franchisee. He seemed successful in his other business ventures, so I visited him and agreed to sell him the right to develop at least two franchises within two years. Unfortunately, he didn't open any locations as planned. After two years, we ended our agreement and continued our business.

While in Canada for the conference, we met Bruce, who attended our meeting in Cincinnati. We signed a franchise agreement with Bruce for Gainesville, Florida, which quickly became operational.

Craig, who was teaching at Hondros College, met Richard in his class in 2008. Richard had his business cards and marketing materials, and he discussed his plan to start a company in Cincinnati with Craig. During their conversation, Richard expressed his interest in buying a franchise as well. However, Craig explained that since our corporate location was already in Cincinnati, we did not have another franchise territory to sell.

Craig and I discussed the situation and decided to meet with Richard. The meeting was successful, and we felt that Richard was the perfect fit to own the franchise in

Cincinnati. Therefore, we sold him the franchise and made him the new owner.

When selecting a franchise partner, it was crucial to find someone who shared our mission of providing education to clients rather than just following a checklist. Craig and I met with Richard to discuss the potential sale of our Cincinnati location, and he impressed us with his attention to detail and thorough questioning. When asked why he wanted to enter the home inspection business, Richard explained his desire to help people navigate one of life's most important purchases. His mission aligned perfectly with ours, and I had complete confidence in his ability to represent our company as a franchise owner. We quickly agreed and sealed the deal with a handshake.

In 2008, we entrusted the attorneys to prepare the necessary paperwork before signing it. This made Richard the franchise owner of Cincinnati, and I became a franchisor as there were no company-owned locations anymore. It was a unique feeling but an exciting one, as we now had the potential to assist others in becoming franchisees and owning their own thriving business. Richard adhered to our established system and increased his business by hiring inspectors like Paul and Carl for Dayton and Ryan for Northern Kentucky. As the business expanded, Carl, John, and Ryan became franchisees of the Dayton, Columbus, and Northern Kentucky markets, respectively. All locations were growing, and additional inspectors were being hired despite the challenges posed by the housing market and the economic downturn. We became the most reliable inspection company in all the markets we were serving.

Through the years, our business underwent significant changes, as any business does. However, we always supported each other during those challenging times. Unfortunately, John, our Columbus franchisee, passed away while he still owned the business. However, one of his inspectors, David, continued the business not only as an opportunity for himself but also to honor John's hard work and efforts in starting the Columbus location.

We achieved organic growth by finding inspectors working for our franchisees who wanted to become franchisees themselves. Soon, four more locations were added in New Jersey, all of which were inspectors for Harish at some point. He mentored and trained them to become their business owners, including John J. in Wall, New Jersey; Diaa A. in Bayonne, New Jersey; Larry G. in Bergen, New Jersey; and Bhavesh, Harish's son, in Cherry Hill, New Jersey. All these locations were under Harish, who was successful in all aspects of the business.

Harish's brother-in-law frequently visited him from Georgia and was impressed with the business and the opportunity it presented. He decided to venture into the business, and a new location opened in Atlanta, Georgia. Our most recent location, in Maineville, Ohio, was opened by an inspector whom I knew from my time as a general contractor when building my home. His name was Marc, and he was one of the electricians in my home construction.

It was my first time experiencing residential ground-up construction, and I learned a lot about the differences between residential and commercial ground-up construction. Anyway, Marc asked me one day how I decided to do the construction on my own, and I told him about the home inspection business and how I had gained a lot of knowledge over the years. He was fascinated by the home inspection industry and asked if we might be hiring. Marc started as an inspector for Richard in Cincinnati and worked for him for almost seven years before he decided to take the plunge and own his franchise location in Maineville, Ohio. Bruce didn't renew his franchise in Gainesville, Florida, after the first five-year term, but the rest of the locations are still up and running. Now, we have a total of 11 locations as of September 2023.

"The journey of a thousand miles begins with a single step."

- Lao Tzu

Chapter 13: Becoming a Hotelier

Back in 2008, when I sold the Cincinnati location to Richard, it freed me up to start looking at other business ventures. One of my close friends, Sam, who I met at a networking event for Indian people when I first moved to Cincinnati, asked me if I would be interested in building a hotel. At first, I said no way, as my past experiences were not good, and I didn't want to end up in the same situation again. He also didn't want to manage the hotel and suggested we develop a hotel together and then partner with a management company so that they could manage the hotel.

I liked the idea and told him that we could look into that. We ventured up to Columbus, Ohio, and started looking for a site in the Easton Town Center area. We came across a site that was for sale, contacted the broker, and found out that the site was worth $1 million.

As we were putting together our numbers to place an offer, someone else placed an offer, and just like that, we were out of the running for that site. We started going to some hotel conferences as we were determined to find something in the area. We continued looking for additional sites and came across a few other locations, but they were either going to be difficult or more expensive.

One day, as we were driving around, we saw a new "for sale" sign at the original site that we had looked at. It had a different phone number and name for the seller this time. We called and found out that the bank had foreclosed on the previous owner, and now the bank was selling the land. We asked the broker how much they were looking for, and he said $325K, and they had just listed it a few days ago. We immediately made an offer, and it was accepted; the only caveat was that we had no time to do due diligence, and we had to close in 30 days. So, my friends Sam and Bob, whom I had known for years, got the money together and took down the land.

It was a big risk as we didn't know if we would get the zoning changes and didn't know if there were any underlying conditions with the land. We jokingly had said that if it didn't work out, our wives would probably divorce us, and we would end up building a house there for the three of us. Thankfully, that wasn't the case.

As we started the process, we met a general contractor who had a lot of experience with difficult sites. He helped us get started with the site. It was a brutal process as we had to go in for a public hearing to have the site transitioned from residential to commercial, and there was some opposition, but we finally got the site approved. We also discovered that the previous owner had destroyed some of the wetlands, and we would have to restore that. Along with the fact that there was no sewer at the site, we had to bring a sewer to the site.

As we were working through these challenges, we went to several conferences for hotels. We went to the Hunter Hotel Investment Conference in Atlanta, Georgia. We met many people at the conference, and the last morning we were there, we went for breakfast and sat at a table where we met

Claude and Glenn. They had a development and management company in Kentucky, and we told them about our site. They were intrigued by our story and told us to contact them once everything was resolved with the land, sewer, and zoning.

We complied, and once everything with the land was sorted, we met with them again and began our partnership. We decided to build a Holiday Inn Express & Suites by IHG as there were no IHG hotels in the Easton Town Center area, and there were multiple Hilton and Marriott properties. This would give us the ability to service the loyal IHG rewards members who were coming to the area. We then hired a general contractor who offered design-building services, and we thought that would be a good fit as they had worked with challenging sites previously.

As we were going through the design process, we realized that with the amount of land we could develop, we would only be able to build 80 rooms, and we needed to build 100 rooms to make it a viable and profitable business option. John, who was with the general contractor, was quite creative and had a great idea to get some additional land from an adjacent church next door. We approached the church as they had extra land and worked out a deal to purchase a quarter acre from them so that we could add the 20 rooms needed to make it a 100-room hotel.

The church was grateful that we could help them out; in return, they could help us; it was a win-win situation. Once we completed the design and our construction budget, we went out to get financing. This was shortly after the 2008 recession, so we ended up doing an SBA Loan, which was not fun. It was a lot of extra paperwork and fees, but we didn't have a choice. We closed on the loan and started construction. It took about 12 months to build the hotel. Sam and I made many trips up to the site, and we had some great times. We opened the hotel, which was a great success.

Shortly after, I found some land in New Albany and decided to build a Hampton Inn and started the entire process. We built the hotel, and things were really starting to look up for me. Around this time, another great friend, Girish, whom I had met years ago in Ohio, had moved to Phoenix and started up a hotel real estate brokerage company and asked if I would help him out with a hotel that was just minutes from my house and needed a court-appointed receiver. I didn't really know what that meant, so I Googled it and found out that when a hotel isn't performing well and may be in the process of being foreclosed on, the bank had the right to appoint a receiver to take over the asset on behalf of the borrower and run it until it gets to the point of break-even or profitable or can be sold to get the debt satisfied.

I told Girish I had no desire to run a hotel, but he insisted and said it would only be for a couple of weeks as they already had a buyer for it, so I agreed to do it.

I went to court and took the oath to run the property until it was sold. Well, I didn't realize what I was truly getting myself into, and when I went to the hotel to let the current owner know that they had to relinquish all control and leave the property, the owner was a family with young children and it was a tough situation to ask someone to leave the property. I did it as delicately as I could and took over the operations of the hotel. It was a small 50-room hotel run by the family, and they didn't have any staff. Here I was, running a hotel without any staff and reliving my younger years and the Colorado days of running a hotel. It was not a fun time.

The potential buyer came in the following week, looked around, and left. Shortly after that, I received a call from Girish, and he said the buyer backed out and didn't want to buy the hotel. So here I am, working in the hotel and managing it day to day, working the front desk, making rooms, and keeping the hotel operating. During this time, I was staying in touch with my friend Jed, whom I had met at Bally's, and he asked me why I didn't want to do the receivership and management. I told him how I really enjoyed starting up businesses and developing hotels but wasn't too excited about the day-to-day operations. Well, he was an operations guy, and he said he would enjoy doing the operations. We discussed his moving to Mason and starting up the management division for Crestpoint.

He moved in at the end of December 2011, and in January 2012, we started the management company. We were working out of a room in the hotel that I was managing as a receiver, and after changing the flag of the hotel, we sold it on behalf of the bank, and word started spreading about our ability to turn around the hotel. We started marketing to lenders that had hotel loans to let them know about our receivership services, and we started picking up additional receiverships and continued to grow that division of our company. Soon after, we received a phone call from the owner of a hotel in Elizabethtown, Kentucky. They had recently acquired a Quality Inn and were looking for a management company, and Choice Hotels recommended us to them. We drove in to visit the two owners, toured the property, and gave them our proposal to manage the hotel for them as a third-party management company. They were impressed by us and hired us. We later found out that they had called a few other companies, but we were the only ones who made a trip to see the hotel and learn about the market and their vision and goals.

During the meeting, we asked them about their goals, and they said they were long-term asset holders. I did ask if they would consider selling the property, and they said if someone offered the "right amount," they would sell. I asked them to write that number down so that when someone offers that amount, they don't have to get their emotions involved and that, as a business transaction, they can just make the decision since they were offered the amount they had written down.

Jed stayed down in Elizabethtown for weeks at a time to get everything rolling and hire everyone, as well as help with their renovation plans and oversee the renovations. The owners were happy with our performance. This continued to help us get additional hotel owners to have us manage their hotels as third-party managers. We hired some support staff and purchased an office condo in Mason to have a base of operations.

It was truly an organic growth, and it was an incredible feeling knowing that we were helping so many hotel owners, employees, and guests. Overall, we successfully took over five additional hotels as court-appointed receivers and managed a few additional hotels as third party managers.

"Incredible things in the business world are never made by a single person, but by a team."

- Steve Jobs

Chapter 14: Development

Deciding to expand our business, we started looking for new sites to build a hotel. A friend of mine visited a location near an outdoor mall, the Liberty Centre, built in 2015. However, he didn't end up pursuing it, and therefore, I opted to pursue the site instead.

It was a bit early to settle with the development process, but the developer was the same one that constructed Easton Town Center in Columbus. Hence, I entrusted the developers' vision for Liberty Town Center not to disappoint. Upon researching different franchises, I chose to develop a Home2Suites by Hilton. It was a great concept geared to extended-stay travelers and was bound to thrive in the market as it was a new extended-stay product backed by Hilton.

After purchasing the land, I reached out to a dear friend in Atlanta, collaborating with him to start the execution process. We laid the foundations of the hotel package and were prepared to present it to many potential investors. The investors and partners within our network of acquaintances saw the potential in our project, and we were able to raise enough capital for financing. The next step was to commence the agricultural drawings; the primary objective was obtaining the necessary permits to start the construction.

I met Tony while building the Holiday Inn Express and the Hampton Inn. He was an architect working under Jeff, another great associate, who owned an architectural firm in

Columbus. Jeff had initially helped us with the interior design package for our Holiday Inn Express in Columbus and the Hampton Inn in New Albany. Satisfied with our collaboration, we remained in close contact for future endeavors.

Similar to Jeff, Tony proved to be a wonderful colleague. After Jeff closed his business down, Tony worked for another architecture firm in Columbus. I asked him why he didn't have his own business, to which he replied that he preferred being involved with the actual work of being an architect instead of a 'business owner.'

I assured him that I would support the start of his company and hire him for future projects that would come my way as long as he continued to produce great architectural drawings for the projects. He agreed to design the Home2Suites development as his first project for his own company.

Next, I had to search for a general contractor. During my research, I met Dale, who had extensive experience building hotels in the area. We quickly became acquaintances, and I asked his company to construct the hotel. The process was a success, and we hosted the opening of the hotel within a year.

Simultaneous to this project, I was observing additional locations and discovered many sites. Dale also introduced me to his family. Stephanie, his daughter, was the company president. After conversing with them, we continued to maintain both our business relationship and friendship.

I'm so thankful for my business ventures, which enabled me to foster incredible associations. It was quite rewarding to look for sites while learning all the different franchises and flags in the market. In 2016, I discovered two locations, one in Wilder, Kentucky, and the other in Cincinnati, Ohio. The site in Cincinnati was a location I desperately wanted to utilize; however, at the time, there was hardly any land available that fit my requirements.

I decided to search for locations in Madisonville, a suburb of Cincinnati, where I met up with John, the landowner of several plots. He advised me to look at some land in Monroe, Ohio, instead, but I felt as though that market was not prepared for another hotel at that time.

After persisting to visit the areas John owned, we started our search with places near Madisonville. He informed me that the land he owned was zoned light industrial, but I had a vision and pursued the site. John, while owning the land, also had a construction company that he owned and operated. He proposed to be the partner for this project and contribute the land as equity. He also requested to act as the contractor to build the hotel.

After hosting an official meeting and performing our due diligence, we came toward a negotiation, becoming partners in the construction of a Holiday Inn Express & Suites at that location.

At the same time, I still had the site at Wilder, Kentucky, but I decided against proceeding with both projects all at once as I didn't want to overwhelm myself. Instead, I met up with a pair of young entrepreneurs looking to enter the hospitality industry but weren't sure where to start.

Having previously established several subways and liquor stores, they had no experience in the process of constructing a hotel. They requested my guidance with building a Holiday Inn Express & Suites in Middletown, Ohio, and I gladly obliged. After considering their ideas, I advised them that the site they had decided on initially was not feasible for their project. I presented the location available in Wilder, Kentucky, as an alternative, which they liked, and they decided to move forward with developing it.

Even though it was a place I had reserved for my ventures, I willingly handed it over to the two entrepreneurs and their families as a way to "pay it forward" (the words my mentor Craig had told me previously) to help them start their journey into the hotel business.

About a month later, they asked me to develop and manage the hotel for up to three years so they could learn the process and one day do it themselves. Pleased with the request, I agreed to support them and got hired to be a third-party developer and manager. Despite it being my first time doing third-party development, I made my greatest effort to walk them through the process of financing, purchasing the land, acquiring the franchise agreement, and taking them through the entire process of building the hotel and opening it and managing it for them.

They weren't aware of the full process, so I made sure to lay down the foundations for their understanding. Looking at how much they appreciated my guiding them, I was satisfied with my decision to help them.

We ended up starting both projects simultaneously. I appointed Dale to construct the hotel for them while I oversaw the development process. I found it quite challenging to manage my personal development as well as the third party, but I was determined to build both. So, with the help of my eminent colleagues, we managed to establish both hotels in 2017, a year after the start of construction.

During that time, I stumbled upon another site in Lexington, Kentucky, and decided to build a Fairfield Inn & Suites. The construction for this project began in late 2017, and within thirteen months, the hotel was opened to the public. However, this venture brought problems with the construction. During the early stages of development, I hired a different architect based on the recommendation of one of my previous partners. I regret ever having made that decision.

Even though the newly hired architect was a Lexington local and more feasible for us, he ended up sizing the steel inaccurately. Though it got approved by the brand, city, and engineers, it cost me time and money to get it modified. I vowed never to hire another architect again, having Tony oversee the work again as he assisted in fixing the complications in Lexington and getting the hotel open in time.

Around this time, Chris from Elizabethtown reached out to me. When he hired me to manage his hotel before, I suggested that he write down the price he would sell his hotel to avoid any personal emotions from getting in the way of the right thing to do for the business. He remembered my suggestion and called me to let me know that he had successfully sold his Quality Inn. Moreover, he was looking for a partner to build a new hotel in Elizabethtown and wanted to see if I would be interested. Knowing about the demand in the market, I agreed to find land to construct a Springhill Suites by Marriott.

Chris introduced me to Rick, the landowner, to negotiate for the land. He committed to contributing his land as equity to the project, so we started the development process in 2018 and established the hotel in 2019. As we were finishing the construction in Elizabethtown, Chris recommended that I make a trip to Bardstown, Kentucky, as it was an excellent area to potentially develop a new hotel.

Driving to Bardstown, I observed that it was quite small, which made me skeptical about the location. However, after speaking to the local residing communities, I discovered a hidden gem, a diamond among rocks, and started to do some thorough research.

By hiring a feasibility company, just as I do on every site, I couldn't help but be in awe of the beauty of that town as I started looking for some land fit for a hotel. Amidst my research, I reached out to a landowner who owned a large amount of land in Bardstown. We met officially in a meeting and negotiated out terms, explaining the process of construction.

Similar to Rick from Elizabethtown, who was the landowner for the Springhill, they asked to become partners by contributing the land for equity. I readily agreed, coming to terms with our agreement, and started the building process of the Fairfield Inn & Suites by Marriott, opening it in 2020.

During the Bardstown process, John from Madisonville, Ohio, brought up the Monroe, Ohio, site and inquired if we could collaborate with that development, contributing the land as he did previously with the Holiday Inn Express. After we collaborated on the structure of the deal, we started that project simultaneously with Bardstown, establishing it in 2020 as well. However, in March of the same year, midway through our construction process, we were hit with the Covid 19 pandemic. While it was a challenging feat, we managed to complete both projects on time and within budget.

Still, because of the lockdown and travel being prohibited, we struggled with the opening, but due to our strong associations with our lenders, we survived the pandemic and operated our hotels through a black swan event that no one could ever be prepared for.

Over the years, I had the opportunity to look at many prospects, some in many different corners of the world. From Texas to Tennessee to Illinois, I had many opportunities arriving at my desk, and I enjoyed reviewing all of them, even if, by the end, I didn't want to develop them. It was always rewarding for me to learn about the pros and cons of each site and how it would be ideal for business.

Overseeing other opportunities, from office buildings to storage buildings, I find it all very fascinating and a great way of continuing my learning.

"Business opportunities are like buses; there's always another one coming."

- Richard Branson

Chapter 15: Giving Back

My parents repeatedly emphasized the importance of being a part of the Indian community. They instilled the teachings of always giving back, contributing through charitable donations, or doing 'seva,' the Sanskrit word for the acts of selfless service.

Growing up in this close-knit community, I watched my parents involve themselves in celebrating all the cultural events and Indian holidays. I remember hearing stories about how life was challenging back when my parents were growing up. They had to face financial and personal issues, but they could overcome all the adversities because of the constant support of the community. Without their encouragement, my parents would not have been able to leave India and move to America, a place that provided their kids with a better education and endless opportunities to learn and grow.

The Indian community helped us foster many friends and lifelong companions who continued to support us even after we had left. One such moment was when we were traveling from Canada to California; I recall staying in multiple motels of people my parents knew from India. At times, they weren't even close companion but rather a friend of a friend from our village or the neighboring ones that would take us in, accepting us like family in their homes during our travels.

This continued throughout our move from California to Oklahoma, Colorado, and then to Ohio. To give back to their kindness, when we would stay with a friend or relative during vacation, we would help them run their business by providing aid in manageable tasks in their hotels or motels.

My dad often volunteered in local communities, playing the Indian drums or 'tabla' at all the traditional events. At the same time, my mother would help cook food to satisfy the hundreds of people attending and volunteering. This was a long-time custom passed on for many generations. Although I tried my best to help in any way I could when I was young, the teachings only fell in place after my wife and I became parents and wanted to reciprocate the support of our Indian community and the local community in Mason.

Involving ourselves in the local Indian Temple, we would go there every Sunday to make donations and perform 'seva' whenever we were able to. In 2005, during Hurricane Katrina, I volunteered under FEMA to assess property damages caused by the natural disaster. This was a very eye-opening experience. Since I was volunteering under an organization, I was able to get to the areas prohibited by the general public. I witnessed firsthand the phenomenal job of the government with the recovery efforts, assessing the damage and helping people get back on their feet.

My wife and I were always enthusiastic about the school and extracurricular opportunities of our daughters, Dharma and Saiya. Even before our two girls were born, my wife was a helper at Junior Achievement and often went to school to teach finance. She would visit many local schools in Cincinnati and Mason, teaching their 5th graders and above, working in every way she could alongside me to support our daughters' dreams.

My eldest child, Dharma, showed a keen interest in learning gymnastics, while my younger daughter, Saiya, was interested in competitive jump rope. During Saiya's first year on the team, I would habitually volunteer to help out. Watching the team practice, I quickly noticed the impact sports had on all the children in the team. They learned team spirit, being leaders, working and competing with a team, and supporting their peers simultaneously. Their team-building exercises were unlike any I had ever seen before.

The head coach at the time was Mike, who presented me with an opportunity to be a coach. I quickly denied it without a second thought, saying I did not have any experience as a coach and didn't know anything about competitive jump rope. However, he batted away my reasoning by saying if I could manage people and run a business, I could be a coach. This was an interesting comparison, so I decided to observe a few practices to learn the rules of this sport, and by Saiya's second year, I was an assistant coach.

Soon after that, Dharma also joined their teams, and it became effortless and pleasant to spend time with my girls while coaching all of the kids. This proved to be challenging, though, because I did not want the other students to think that I was playing favorites by only teaching my kids. If my children had any problem regarding this, I would talk to them as a parent and tell them to discuss any issue with the other coaches.

They did not understand why I had asked them to do so, but as they grew older, the realization seemed to dawn upon them, and they accepted my reasoning. My wife, Lina, and I became very involved, enabling us to volunteer at different workshops and travel with the team, becoming very close to the other kids and their parents.

As I figured out where I stood as an assistant coach, I started gravitating more towards motivational and life coaching rather than jump rope coaching. I did spend a reasonable amount of time teaching sports, but most of it would be spent speaking with the other kids. Our conversations ranged from how they were doing at school to what where their future plans were after they had graduated high school. This became a common practice, and soon, I was taking seniors out for coffee conversations to learn about their studies and career plans. I simultaneously also learned a lot from my students. Deep down, I genuinely believe that I helped some of them see things they mightn't have seen otherwise.

Though my girls have now graduated high school and are no longer part of the team, I still continue to be an assistant coach while working as a board member for our non-profit team. A lineup specifically designed to make an impact on many students.

Soon after, I was invited by the Leuva Patidar Samaj, LPS, to speak about my entrepreneurial journey, which I gladly accepted. The LPS of the USA is an organization mainly comprising the members of Leuva Patidar people of predominantly Hindu faith, originating from Navsati, Surat, Tapi, Bharuch, and Valsad districts who settled in the United States.

Sitting among a panel of people from multiple industries was a rewarding experience. Being able to share our career expeditions, answer any questions our audience might have about navigating through the decisions and challenges they may face, and provide some guidance to them was extremely worthwhile.

Our commitment to giving back extended beyond our cultural community. My wife's involvement with the Mason School was another example of how we always looked to give back and help our local community. To help with the visionary ideas and operational agendas they wanted to implement across the schooling district, my wife took leave from Accenture during Saiya's freshman and Dharma's sophomore year of high school. She worked directly for Jonathan, the superintendent of the school.

She really enjoyed helping with such an impactful project while being present with both her kids and their teachers, as well as other students, getting to know them as more than mere acquaintances. Lina, ever the hard worker, continued to work for the Junior Achievement board and the Mason School Foundation Board, helping them with the grant writing committee and the school drive.

Since then, I have been presented with the opportunity to speak at several events, including the Indian American Chamber of Cincinnati, where I was able to share my journey and help others discover what theirs might look like. In 2023, I was asked by one of the assistant coaches from the Mason Comet Skippers, who is now involved with Mason Schools as the Experimental Experience Coordinator, to be a speaker about entrepreneurship. Pleased with the proposition, I gladly accepted.

All in all, I have spoken in many classes, sophomores, juniors, and seniors, and it was quite pleasant to recall all of my expeditions and the challenges I faced along the way, helping them understand what it means to be an entrepreneur. Most recently, I have been introduced to the position of a board member for the West Chester Liberty Chamber Alliance, and I aspire to add value to this local community.

"Always give without remembering and always receive without forgetting."

-Brian Tracy

Chapter 16: Passion and Grit

People often ask me how I juggle so many responsibilities—running businesses, being active in the community, and still finding time for my family. The secret really comes down to understanding my "why." Whenever I take on a new project, I'm motivated by the chance to solve problems and create opportunities, whether it's for my business or my career.

My family—my wife, daughters, parents, and grandparents—are at the heart of everything I do. They inspire me and drive my passion. Whether it's spending hours coaching my daughters' jump rope team or serving on a community board, it's all about making their world a better place.

So when people ask, "How do you manage it all?" I tell them it's not about the logistics or time management. It's about knowing your purpose and what truly motivates you. My parents taught me from a young age that understanding what drives you is what really matters.

For me, the "why" is clear. It's the joy I see in my daughters' eyes when they succeed, the satisfaction of making a positive impact in my community, and the fulfillment I get from my work and businesses. This "why" acts as my compass, helping me navigate the busy and sometimes chaotic aspects of managing responsibilities.

Finding your own “why” isn’t always easy. It takes introspection, self-reflection, and a willingness to dig deep to discover your true purpose. It means asking yourself tough questions: What brings me joy? What am I passionate about? What kind of legacy do I want to leave? What is my purpose?

Take time to explore your passions, reflect on your values, and listen to your heart. Your “why” might not come to you immediately, but with patience and persistence, you will find what truly drives you. Whether through journaling, meditation, or seeking advice from mentors, there are many ways to embark on this journey of discovering your purpose. I encourage you to join me in this quest. Let’s unlock the power of purpose together and reach our full potential.

Many people struggle with the idea of shortcuts to success—they want to achieve more while working less. But that’s not how success works. If you’re aiming to reach your goals, you need to be ready to put in the effort and embrace hard work, determination, discipline, commitment, and sacrifice.

Ask yourself: Are you truly willing to go all in? How much do you really want to succeed? Nothing of value comes easily, and success isn’t a matter of luck. Even if you’re incredibly talented, you won’t reach your goals without putting in the work. That’s why grit is so important—it’s the foundation of success.

The good news is that grit can be developed over time. But to build it, you need to adopt a growth mindset. Many people have a fixed mindset, but those who are passionate about their goals understand their values, beliefs, and needs deeply. They live in alignment with their true selves and inspire others to do the same.

Living with passion means paying attention to what makes you come alive and following that path.

Not everyone will understand the path you choose in life, and that's perfectly okay. True grit means tuning out others' judgments and staying focused on your own journey. I've never met a strong person who didn't face significant challenges. Perseverance is about facing your struggles head-on and learning to embrace the discomfort that comes with them.

The difference between those who succeed and those who don't often comes down to their willingness to keep going despite setbacks. It's about having a burning desire to achieve your dreams, no matter the obstacles.

Embrace discomfort and use it as a tool for growth. Celebrate every achievement along the way, and don't stop until you're genuinely proud of who you've become. Gritty people are resilient; they thrive through adversity, viewing every challenge as an opportunity to grow. They work to master their emotions and keep pushing forward, even when others give up.

Resilience isn't just about being tough; it's about the willingness to keep trying and adapting when things get tough. Resilient people know when to accept life's ups and downs and make space for new possibilities.

The quickest way to master anything is through practice and repetition. To build perseverance, you need to step out of your comfort zone and try new things. This is how you develop grit. Grit is about the daily habits you build—consistently doing what you know will lead to success. The more you invest in your personal growth, the more skilled you'll become and the better you'll be at what you do. Gritty people live intentionally.

Over the past 30 years, I've read many books, but one that stands out is Angela Duckworth's Grit: The Power of Passion and Perseverance. Duckworth's research on 16,000 people revealed that those with more grit are often driven to live a meaningful, other-centered life. When you face obstacles, reconnect with your "why." It's what will keep you moving forward, even when you feel like giving up. When challenges arise, do you let them stop you, or do you use those moments to push yourself to grow stronger? Gritty people face challenges head-on and keep going until they succeed.

Remember, the only real failure is quitting. Life is messy, and failure is part of the journey. What matters is how you respond to it. It's okay to fall down seven times as long as you get back up on the eighth. If you master the art of never giving up, there's no limit to what you can achieve. You have one life—make it a masterpiece. The only limits are the ones you set in your mind. Master your mind, and you master your life. Never give up on your dreams. Strive to be gritty in every area of your life, and your future self will thank you.

"It was passion and perseverance that made high achievers special. In a word, they had grit."

-Angela Duckworth

Chapter 17: Conclusion

I'm sure many of you are wondering what I am doing today. So, I want to update you on what I've been working on recently. My younger daughter Saiya and I co-founded a social media ad agency called SocialSaiya in 2021. Our journey began when I was dissatisfied with the social media marketing for 1st Inspection Services. The agency managing our posts used generic content, like palm tree images for our New Jersey locations, which didn't fit our brand.

Seeing the need for a more tailored approach, I asked Saiya and my other daughter to help with creating and posting content. They did a great job with both content creation and branding. However, individual posting on each location's Facebook and Instagram accounts was time-consuming.

To streamline the process, I looked into platforms that could manage multiple accounts and offer additional features like scheduling posts and responding to reviews. After finding a suitable platform, Saiya and I decided to start SocialSaiya. We began by managing the social media for 1st Inspection Services and our hotels. As word spread, other businesses noticed, and we now have over 20 clients.

We've also attended various industry conferences, where we've shared our expertise and helped other businesses with their social media marketing. SocialSaiya currently employs several high school and college students, and we're excited about our continued growth. It's been a rewarding experience working with Saiya, and she has learned a lot about business planning, pitch decks, P&L statements, and various industries.

In 2020, my mom passed away during the COVID-19 pandemic, which was incredibly difficult for our family. She was our biggest supporter and the one who kept us all together. Her loss was deeply felt by our family and our community. My father is still with us, but both he and I carry the pain of her absence.

About a year after her passing, my wife Lina, our daughters Dharma and Saiya, and I were preparing for a trip to Hawaii. We needed negative COVID tests to board the flight, but the tests Lina and Dharma had taken at a local drug store were not processed correctly, and our flight was in 48 hours. Our friends in Denver suggested we go to AFC Urgent Care, an urgent care that offers rapid COVID testing. I initially had trouble finding a location in Mason, but we eventually got the tests done at a different clinic, and we made our trip to Hawaii.

While on vacation, I noticed a "Become a Franchisee" link on the AFC Urgent Care website. This piqued my interest, so I spent the next three months researching the possibility of becoming an AFC Urgent Care franchisee. After thorough research and discussions with my business partners, we saw an opportunity in the urgent care sector. We felt that many urgent care centers lacked a sense of hospitality and were often too sterile.

We visited several AFC Urgent Care locations in North Carolina and Tennessee, spoke with owners and operators, and realized this could be a chance to improve medical care with a more welcoming approach. We decided to open our first AFC Urgent Care location in West Chester, Ohio. Though I didn't become a doctor, this was a way to provide care to the community, something my mom always wanted for me.

We've since opened a second location in Oakley/Hyde Park. The healthcare industry is challenging, but we've learned a lot and continue to grow. It's been a tough but rewarding journey, and I like to think my mom would be proud of what we're doing.

When we started the West Chester location, we needed to build out the leased space. My partners trusted me to take on the role of general contractor due to my experience in development. So, I decided to start a general construction company. I managed to complete the build-out on time and within budget, and both my partners and AFC Corporate were pleased with the results.

Following this success, I took on the build-out for our second location, again completing it on time and within budget. Currently, I'm preparing for a new project: a Hampton Inn & Suites in Bardstown, Kentucky, which is set to begin construction in the Spring of 2025.

I've had a few other requests to bid on construction projects, but I've learned to be selective about the projects I take on. I plan to work on only a few projects moving forward.

Over the years, I've realized that I have a strong passion for solving problems and helping people. This drive motivates me every day and is a major source of my personal growth. Looking back, I never imagined owning and running multiple businesses across different industries, but my enthusiasm for finding solutions where others see obstacles has been a key factor in my journey.

My purpose lies in service—addressing people's needs and overcoming challenges. There's a special satisfaction in finding solutions when others believe there are none, and this has become my mission. I believe everyone should find their purpose or "why." Discovering this provides direction and fuels determination. But finding your purpose is just the start. Once you have it, you need to be ready to work hard, face obstacles, and persist no matter what.

In my experience, problem-solving is more than just finding answers; it's about building resilience and creativity. When someone brings me a problem, I always ask them to come back with at least three potential solutions. Often, one of those solutions will be the key to overcoming the challenge. This approach requires deep thinking, critical analysis, and a willingness to invest time and effort.

Success is a personal journey and is defined by your own standards, not by others. It's about setting your own goals, working hard to achieve them, and finding satisfaction in the process. I encourage everyone to discover their own purpose, commit to their goals, and embrace the hard work involved. When you do this, you'll find that success is not only possible but also likely.

"If you don't have purpose,
then the passion doesn't ignite."

-Kal Patel

Made in the USA
Columbia, SC
01 February 2025

751f303f-2a1a-4905-a847-dc5dda8568ffR01